About this series...

Series Editors: Mark L. Knapp & John A. Daly,
both at the University of Texas

Designed for college and university undergraduates, the **Interpersonal Commtexts** series will also interest a much larger general audience. Ideal as basic or supplementary texts, these volumes are suited for courses in the development and practice of interpersonal skills; verbal and nonverbal behavior (the basis of interpersonal transactions); functions of communication in face-to-face interaction; the development of interpersonal behavior at various points in the lifespan; and intergroup and intercultural aspects of interpersonal communication. Readable and comprehensive, the **Interpersonal Commtexts** describe contexts within which interpersonal communication takes place and provide ways to study and understand the interpersonal communication process.

In this series...

Bridging
Differences

Effective Intergroup Communication

William B. Gudykunst

INTERPERSONAL COMMTEXTS 3

SAGE PUBLICATIONS
The International Professional Publishers
Newbury Park   London   New Delhi

For information address:

SAGE Publications, Inc.
2455 Teller Road
Newbury Park, California 91320

SAGE Publications Ltd.
6 Bonhill Street
London EC2A 4PU
United Kingdom

SAGE Publications India Pvt. Ltd.
M-32 Market
Greater Kailash I
New Delhi 110 048 India

Printed in the United States of America

Library of Congress Cataloging-in-Publication Data

Gudykunst, William B.
    Bridging differences: effective intergroup communication / William B. Gudykunst.
        p.   cm. — (Interpersonal commtexts ; v. 3)
    Includes bibliographical references and index.
    ISBN 0-8039-3330-4 — ISBN 0-8039-3331-2 (pbk.)
    1. Intercultural communication. I. Title. II. Series.
    HM258.G838   1991
    303.48′2—dc20   90-24108
                                                            CIP

FIRST PRINTING, 1991

Sage Production Editor: Astrid Virding

Contents

Preface

I originally became involved in studying "intercultural" communication in the United States Navy when I served as an "Intercultural Relations Specialist" in Japan. We designed and conducted training to help naval personnel and their families adjust to living in Japan. While conducting intercultural training in Japan, I thought "intercultural" communication (i.e., communication between people from different cultures) was different from "intracultural" communication (i.e., communication with members of our own culture).

After getting out of the Navy, I went to Minnesota to study for my Ph.D. with Bill Howell. While completing my Ph.D., I continued to see intercultural communication as different from intracultural communication. I also remained interested in training and applications while working on my Ph.D. After accepting a position as an Assistant Professor, however, I focused on conducting research and developing theory. Over the next 10 years, I developed the theory of interpersonal and intergroup communication on which this book is based.

In trying to develop a way to explain communication between people from different cultures, I came to see that the variables operating when we communicate interculturally are the same as when we communicate intraculturally. I, therefore, now see the *process* underlying intercultural and intracultural communication to be the same. To illustrate, our stereotypes always affect our communication. Stereotypes, however, lead to ineffective communication more frequently when the person with whom we are communicating comes from another culture than when the person comes from our own culture. One reason for this is that our stereotypes of our culture tend to be more "accurate" and "favorable" than our stereotypes of other cultures. "Inaccurate" and "unfavorable" stereotypes of other cultures and ethnic groups cause us to misinterpret messages we receive from members of those cultures and ethnic groups.

Given that the underlying process of communication is the same in intercultural and intracultural encounters, we need a way to refer to this common underlying process. Young Yun Kim and I used "communicating with strangers" to refer to this common process in our intercultural communication text (Gudykunst & Kim, 1984; Kim & Gudykunst, in press). I have drawn on the framework in *Communicating with Strangers* and the work of Harry Triandis, Howard Giles, Charles Berger, and Walter Stephan to develop a theory designed to explain interpersonal and intergroup communication (intercultural communication is a type of intergroup communication). I apply this theory and Ellen Langer's work on mindfulness to improving communication effectiveness in this book. While my emphasis is on improving communication effectiveness with people from different cultures and ethnic groups, the ideas can be applied to communication with people from our own culture and ethnic group as well.

I wrote the book for anyone who is interested in improving his or her communication with people from other cultures or ethnic groups. The book should be useful to undergraduate students in a variety of courses, including interpersonal or intercultural communication, intergroup relations, management, social work, nursing, criminal justice, and tourism, to name only a few. The book also should be useful to members of the general public who work with people from different cultural or ethnic backgrounds, as well as to people traveling to other countries. I have tried to write in a conversational style so that the material will be accessible to as many people as possible. I do *not* assume that you have any prior knowledge of communication in general, or intercultural communication in particular.

There are numerous people who have contributed, either directly or indirectly, to the book. Exposure to Kurt Lewin's writing early in my graduate career convinced me that theories must have practical application. Bill Howell and George Shapiro reinforced this notion at Minnesota. Tsukasa Nishida, Gao Ge, Mitch Hammer, and Karen Schmidt have worked with me on many of the studies on which the theory is based, and Mitch co-authored the special version of the theory applied to intercultural adaptation. Sandy Sudweeks, Paula Trubisky, Joyce Baker, David Doyle, Mark Cole, and I initially applied the theory to designing an intercultural training program. Participants in my "Applications of Intercultural Communication" class at California State University, Fullerton tested many of the ideas I present in the book in training programs they conducted last spring. Stella Ting-Toomey served as a sounding board for the theory and its application. She also read a complete draft of the book and suggested the title. Harry Triandis, Rich Wiseman, Jon Bruschke, and the Series Co-Editors, Mark Knapp and John Daly, also provided valuable feedback on a draft of the book. The book would not have been written without the gentle prodding and encouragement of Ann West, my editor at Sage. Finally, the time to write the book was made possible by a Senior Faculty Research Grant from California State University, Fullerton.

William B. Gudykunst

Greetings! I am pleased
to see that we are different.
May we together become greater
than the sum of both of us.

Vulcan Greeting
(Star Trek)

See at a distance an undesirable person;
See close at hand a desirable person;
Come closer to the undesirable person;
Move away from the desirable person.
Coming close and moving apart,
how interesting life is!

Gensho Ogura

Communicating with Strangers

Most of us have relatively little contact with people from other cultures and/or ethnic groups. Interacting with people who are different is a novel experience for most of us (Rose, 1981). The amount of contact we have with people who are different, however, is going to change in the near future. Recent estimates suggest that the work force in the United States is changing from white, male-dominated to a majority of women, immigrants, and nonwhite ethnics (Hudson Institute, 1987). While organizational cultures influence the way we behave in the workplace, they do not erase the effect of cultural and ethnic background on our behavior at work (Adler, 1986). Most of us recognize "problems" in the workplace due to diversity, but few of us recognize the advantages of a diverse work force.

Lennie Copeland (1988) argues that there are many benefits that cultural and ethnic diversity bring to the workplace. If

1

ropriately, diverse work groups are creative,
elcome new perspectives, and are productive.
o points out that diversity has advantages for
iverse workplaces, for example, provide a place
nces can be discussed, where employees' perspec-
dened, and where employees can learn to enjoy
interacting with people who are different. For these advantages
to occur, however, employees must understand how they communicate with people from other cultures and/or ethnic groups
and why misunderstandings occur.

Many of us believe that misunderstandings in intercultural
and interethnic encounters are due to one of the individuals
not being competent in the other's language. Linguistic knowledge alone, however, is not enough to ensure that our communication with people from other cultures or ethnic groups
will progress smoothly and/or be effective. Confucius said that
"human beings are drawn close to one another by their common
nature, but habits and customs keep them apart." Misunderstandings in intercultural and interethnic encounters often
stem from not knowing the norms and rules guiding the communication of people from different cultures and/or ethnic
groups. If we understand others' languages, but not their cultures, we can make fluent fools of ourselves.

Language and culture are not the only factors that can contribute to misunderstandings in intercultural and interethnic
encounters. Our attitudes (e.g., prejudices) and stereotypes create expectations that often lead us to misinterpret messages
we receive from people who are different *and* lead people
who are different to misinterpret the messages they receive
from us. Spike Lee (1990), Director of the film *Do the Right
Thing,* for example, recently pointed out that expressing "racism is fashionable today." When people express their unconscious racist attitudes toward others, misunderstanding is
inevitable and conflict is probable.

Our expectations regarding how people from other cultures
and/or ethnic groups will behave are based on how we categorize them (e.g., he is Japanese; she is Mexican-American).

Our use of social categories, however, is not limited to our communication with people from different cultures and/or ethnic groups. We categorize others when we communicate with people from our own culture or ethnic group, but the categories are different (e.g., that person is a woman; he is a waiter; she or he is a "friend of a friend").

Until we "know" others, our interactions with them must be based on our expectations regarding how people in the category in which we place them will behave. Our initial interactions with people from our own groups and with people from other groups, therefore, are relatively similar. There are, of course, some differences (e.g., we experience more anxiety when people come from different ethnic groups than when they are from our ethnic group). To be able to talk about the similarities in the underlying communication process, I refer to people who are not members of our own groups and who are "different" (on the basis of culture, ethnicity, gender, age, or other group memberships) as "strangers."[1]

In this book, I draw attention to those factors that are given more weight when we communicate with strangers than with people from our own groups. Our stereotypes, for example, affect our communication with people from our own groups and our communication with strangers. Stereotypes are, however, less "problematic" in our communication with people from our own groups because our stereotypes of our own groups usually are more favorable and "accurate" than our stereotypes of other groups. In order to improve our effectiveness in communicating with strangers, we must understand how "unfavorable" and/or inaccurate stereotypes affect the way we communicate.

Improving our communication with strangers requires that we become aware of how we communicate. William Howell (1982) argues that awareness and competence can be thought of as a four stage process:[2] (1) "unconscious incompetence" where we misinterpret others' behavior, but are not aware of it; (2) "conscious incompetence" where we are aware that we misinterpret others' behavior, but we do not do anything about it; (3) "conscious competence" where we think about our communication behavior and consciously modify it to improve our effectiveness (I refer to this stage as "mindfulness" below); and (4) "un\conscious competence" where we have practiced the skills for effective communication to the extent that we no longer have to think about them to use them.

We have a responsibility to deal with cultural and ethnic differences in a constructive fashion.

Throughout the book, I point out areas where we are unconsciously incompetent in communicating with strangers and provide suggestions on how we can become consciously competent. Moving to the level of unconscious competence requires practicing the skills discussed in the book. Once we have mastered the skills, conscious attention gets in the way of effective communication and takes away from enjoying our communication with strangers (Spitzberg & Cupach, 1984).

I have drawn on a theory of interpersonal and intergroup communication I have been developing over the last several years (the most recent version is Gudykunst, 1988) and recent work on "mindfulness" (Langer, 1989) in cognitive psychology in writing the book.[3] Kurt Lewin often is quoted as saying "there is nothing so practical as a good theory." I agree and go a step further. I believe that training and practical "advice" must be theoretically based. While the book is based on a communication theory, I do not present the theory in detail. Rather, I focus on practical applications of the theory. Throughout, I "translate" the theory so that we can use it to improve our abilities to communicate effectively and manage conflict with strangers.

Conflict between people of different ethnic and cultural groups is occurring throughout the world today. Examples of intergroup conflict include, but are not limited to, recent racial harassment on university campuses in the United States, nationality conflicts in the Soviet Union (e.g., between the Azerbaijanis and the Armenians), conflicts between Protestants and Catholics in Northern Ireland, and between Arabs and Jews in Israel, to name only a few.

While the specific "causes" of intergroup conflict differ depending upon the situation, all incidents share one thing in common; namely, they involve "polarized communication." Robert Arnett (1986) argues that

> the major problem of the human community for the remainder of this century and into the next . . . [is] communication from polarized positions. Polarized communication can be summarized as the inability to believe or seriously consider one's view as wrong and the other's opinion as truth. Communication within human community becomes typified by the rhetoric of "we" are right and "they" are misguided or wrong. (pp. 15-16)

Polarized communication, therefore, exists when groups or individuals look out for their own interests and have little concern for others' interests.

Lack of concern for others' interests leads to moral exclusion. "Moral exclusion occurs when individuals or groups are perceived as *outside the boundary in which moral values, rules, and considerations of fairness apply.* Those who are morally excluded are perceived as nonentities, expendable, or undeserving; consequently, harming them appears acceptable, appropriate or just" (Optow, 1990, p. 1). Lack of concern for others and moral exclusion are a function, at least in part, of "spiritual deprivation" (i.e., the feeling of emptiness associated with separation from our fellow humans) that Mother Teresa sees as the major problem facing the world today (Jampolsky, 1989).

There is a tendency for many of us to think that cultural and ethnic diversity inevitably lead to polarized communication. This, however, is not the case. How we deal with cultural and ethic diversity determines the outcome. I contend that we have a responsibility as human beings to try to deal with cultural and ethnic differences in a constructive fashion. This suggests that we have a responsibility to try to communicate effectively with strangers. To communicate effectively, we must try to construct our messages in a way that strangers can understand what we mean and we need to try to interpret strangers' messages to us in the way they meant them to be interpreted. If strangers do not try to communicate effectively with us, it does not relieve us of our responsibility. We also have a responsibility to react when we see others "put down" members of other groups. If we say nothing when we hear someone make a racist or sexist remark, for example, we are equally culpable.

I do *not* mean to suggest that we try to communicate intimately or try to establish a personal relationship with all strangers we meet. This is impossible. We can, however, try to communicate effectively with strangers whatever our relationship (e.g., acquaintance, neighbor, co-worker, superior, subordinate, etc.) with them is. I also am not advocating that we "hit our head against a brick wall." No matter how hard we try, it may be impossible to communicate effectively or establish a cooperative relationship with some people. In cases like this, we each have to make an individual decision when it is time to stop trying. The important thing, in my opinion, is that we *try* to communicate effectively with strangers we meet.

In order to know how to "improve" our communication with strangers, we have to understand our "normal" tendencies when we communicate with them. To help you assess your communication with strangers, I present questionnaires designed to assess your tendencies regarding the major constructs I discuss.[4] Completing the questionnaires is not critical to understanding the material presented, but it will assist you in improving your effectiveness in communicating with strangers. When completing the questionnaires, please keep in mind that they will only help you improve your communication if you answer them honestly.

Given this outline of my approach and the purpose of the book, I will overview the process of communication. In the next section, I examine the role of symbols, messages, and meanings in communication. Following this, I isolate the functions of communication (reducing anxiety and uncertainty) that are central to the theory I use to guide the book. I conclude by looking at some of the factors that have more of an influence on our behavior when we communicate with strangers than when we communicate with people from our own groups.

❏ An Overview of the Communication Process

We all communicate and consider ourselves to be "experts" on the topic.[5] We think we know what the problems are and how to solve them. Unfortunately, many of the things we take for granted about communication lead to ineffective communication, especially when we communicate with strangers.

There are many ways to define communication. If we went to a convention of communication scholars and stopped 10 people at random asking them to define communication, for example, we would probably get 10 different definitions. The view of communication I present in this chapter is only one view.

SYMBOLS AND MESSAGES

Language often is equated with speech and communication.[6] There are, however, important differences. Language is a system of rules regarding how the sounds of the language are made, about how sentences are formed, about the meaning of words or combinations of words, and about how the language is used. Language is a medium of communication. When the rules of language are translated into a channel of communication (e.g., the spoken word) using symbols, messages are created.

Symbols are things we use to represent something else. Virtually anything can be a symbol—words, nonverbal displays, flags, and so forth. Referents for symbols can include objects, ideas, or behaviors. The word "flag," for example, is used to represent a piece of cloth with "stars and stripes" that is attached to a staff and serves as the "national banner" in the United States. As the recent disagreements over the meaning of flag burning indicate, the symbol means different things to different people. For some, it is sacred and should not be burned or devalued under any circumstances. For others, it is not held in such high esteem and burning the flag is an expression of free speech. The point is that there is no natural connection between a specific symbol and its referent. The relationship between a symbol and its referent is arbitrary and varies from culture to culture. It also varies within cultures, as the example of the flag indicates. While there is not a direct relationship between the symbol and its referent, there are direct connections between our thoughts and a symbol and our thoughts and the symbol's referent (Ogden & Richards, 1923). If we think of the referent, the symbol comes to mind; if we think of the symbol, the referent comes to mind.

We combine a set of symbols into messages that we encode to send to others. Encoding involves putting our thoughts, feelings, emotions, and/or attitudes in a form recognizable by others. The encoded messages we create are transmitted to others who decode them. Decoding is the process of perceiving and interpreting the messages and other stimuli from the environment we receive through our senses (seeing, hearing, feeling, touching, smelling, and tasting). How we encode and decode messages is influenced by our life experiences (e.g., our experiences with others, the emotions we have felt). These life experiences include our unique individual experiences, as well as our shared ethnic and cultural experiences. The important point to keep in mind is that no two individuals have *exactly* the same life experiences. No two people, therefore, will interpret a message in the same way.

There are several possible channels of communication through which messages can be transmitted. We can transmit our message through the spoken word, use nonverbal cues, or write it. If one person cannot speak or hear, sign language may be used. Alternatively, messages can be transmitted through mathematics or through artistic forms of expression such as painting, photography, or music. Only when the channel is the spoken word does speech occur.

MESSAGES AND MEANINGS

The term communication refers to the exchange of messages and the creation of meaning (e.g., assigning significance or interpreting the messages). Most communication scholars would agree that meanings cannot be transmitted from one person to another. Only messages can be transmitted. When we send a message we attach a certain meaning to that message and choose the symbols and channel of communication accordingly. The person who receives our message, however, attaches his or her own meaning to the message received. The meaning attached to the message is a function of the message itself, the channel used, the environment in which the message is transmitted, and the person who receives it. Communication is effective to the extent that the other person attaches a meaning to the message similar to what we intended.

We do not send and receive messages independently of one another. We engage in both processes simultaneously. When we encode a message we are affected by how we decode messages we are receiving from the other person and we may even modify our message based on feedback we receive while we are transmitting the message.

We rely on more than the "objective" behavior that the other person displays (e.g., she or he may laugh) when we construct our messages. We also rely on our interpretation of that behavior (e.g., he or she assumes we are funny *or* she or he is laughing at us). The way we construct and interpret messages is a function of our perceptions of ourselves, the other people involved, their "objective" behavior, and the way they send their messages to us.

Paul Watzlawick, Janet Beavin, and Don Jackson (1967) distinguished between the "content" and "relationship" dimensions of a message. Content refers to the information in the message (e.g., what is said). The relationship component of a message is inferred from how the message is transmitted (including the specific words used) and it deals with how the participants are relating to each other. The way we communicate offers a definition of the relationship between us. The children's saying "sticks and stones may break my bones, but names will never hurt me" is not accurate. The words we choose and the way we say them to others can and do hurt.

When we communicate we present ourselves as we want others to see us and respond to how others present themselves to us. We modify how we see ourselves based on the feedback we receive from others.[7] If others consistently tell us we are incompetent, for example, we begin to see ourselves as incompetent. Through communication we can facilitate others' personal growth or destroy them. George Gerbner (1978) refers to the later possibility as "symbolic annihilation."

INTENTION TO COMMUNICATE

Some scholars argue that we must intend to send a message in order to communicate.[8] While this is a viable position, I believe it is overly restrictive and ignores the fact that we often are not highly aware of what our intentions are. One person may not intend to send a message to another person, but the other person may perceive that a message has been sent and react based on his or her interpretation. This is particularly problematic when the people come from different cultures.

Consider an example of a businessperson from the United States negotiating a contract in an Arab culture. During the course of a meeting, the businessperson from the United States crosses her or his legs and in the process points the sole of her or his shoe toward an Arab. The person from the United States, in all likelihood, will not attach any meaning to this. The Arab, in contrast, will probably interpret this behavior as an insult and react accordingly. While the person from the United States did not intend to send a message, one was received. Showing the sole of the foot does not mean anything in the United States. In Arab cultures, however, showing the sole of the foot to another person is considered an insult. The misunderstanding can only be explained by looking at behavior that was not intended to be meaningful.

SOURCES OF COMMUNICATION BEHAVIOR

Our communication behavior is based on one of three sources.[9] First, we engage in much of our communication behavior out of habit. We have learned "scripts" which we enact in particular situations. Scripts are predetermined courses of action we have learned. The greeting ritual is one example. The ritual for greeting others reduces the vast amount of uncertainty and anxiety present in initial interactions with strangers to manageable portions and allows us to interact with others as though there was relatively little uncertainty or anxiety. The norms and rules for the ritual provide us with predictions about how others will respond in the situation. When someone deviates from the script or we enter a new situation, we cannot fall back on the rituals' implicit predictions. Under these circumstances, we actively have to reduce our uncertainty and anxiety before we can make accurate predictions and communicate effectively.

The second basis for our communication behavior is the intentions we form. Intentions are "instructions" we give ourselves about how to communicate (Triandis, 1977). When we think about what we want to do in a particular situation, we form intentions. Intention, therefore, is a cognitive construct— it is part of our thought processes. We may not be able to accomplish our intentions, however. My intention, for example, may be to be nonjudgmental in my interactions with others, but in actuality I may be very judgmental. My ability to accomplish my intentions is a function, at least in part, of my knowledge and skills (discussed in Chapter 6).

The final factor on which our communication behavior may be based is our affect, feelings, or emotions. We often react to others on a strictly emotional basis. If we feel we were criticized, for example, we may become defensive and strike out at the other person without thinking. We can, however, manage our emotional reactions cognitively.[10] In fact, I argue in Chapter 2 that this is necessary for effective communication to occur, especially when we communicate with strangers.

❑ Functions of Communication

There are many reasons why people communicate. We communicate to inform someone about something, to entertain another person, to change another person's attitudes or behavior, and to reinforce our view of ourselves, to name only a few of the possibilities. It is impossible to examine all of the functions in a short book like this. I, therefore, focus on two specific functions that are related closely to effective communication with strangers: reducing uncertainty and anxiety.[11]

Interacting with strangers is a novel situation for most people. "The immediate psychological result of being in a new situation is lack of security. Ignorance of the potentialities inherent in the situation, of the means to reach a goal, and of the probable outcomes of an intended action causes insecurity" (Herman & Schield, 1961, p. 165). Attempts to deal with the ambiguity of new situations involves a pattern of information-seeking (uncertainty reduction) and tension (anxiety) reduction (Ball-Rokeach, 1973).

UNCERTAINTY AND ANXIETY

When we reduce uncertainty about others and ourselves, understanding is possible. Understanding involves obtaining information, knowing, comprehending, and interpreting. Three levels of understanding can be differentiated: description, prediction, and explanation (Berger, Gardner, Parks, Shulman, & Miller, 1976). Description involves delineating what is observed in terms of its physical attributes (i.e., drawing a picture in words). Prediction involves projecting what will happen in a particular situation, while explanation involves stating why something occurred.

We make predictions and create explanations all of the time when we communicate. We rarely describe others' behavior, however. When we communicate with others we typically decode messages by attaching meaning to or interpreting them. We do not stop to describe what we saw or heard before we interpret it. Rather, we interpret messages as we decode them. The problem is that we base our interpretations on our life experiences, culture, or ethnic group memberships. Because our life experiences differ from the other person's, this often leads to misunderstandings. Robin Lakoff (1990) illustrates the problems that emerge when we interpret others' behavior based on our frame of reference:

> We see all behavior from our own internal perspective: what would that mean if *I* did it? And, of course, if I, as a member of my own group, did what that person did in the presence of other members of my group, it would be strange or bad . . . we don't usually extrapolate, we don't say, "Yes, but in *his* [or *her*] frame of reference, what would it mean?" We assume the possibility of direct transfer of meaning, that a gesture or act in Culture A can be understood in the same way by members of Culture B. Often this is true: there are universals of behavior, but as often that is a dangerous assumption; and by cavalierly ignoring the need for translation, we are making misunderstanding inevitable. (pp. 165-166)

Anxiety refers to the feeling of being uneasy, tense, worried, or apprehensive about what might happen. It is an affective (e.g., emotional) response, not a cognitive or behavioral response like uncertainty. While uncertainty results from our inability to predict strangers' behavior, "anxiety stems from the anticipation of negative consequences. People appear to fear at least four types of negative consequences: psychological or behavioral consequences for the self, and negative evaluations by members of the outgroup and the ingroup" (Stephan & Stephan, 1985, p. 159).

Our ingroups are groups with which we identify that are important to us (Triandis, 1988). If we define our religious group as important and identify with being members of our religion, for example, it is one of our ingroups. Other religious groups then become outgroups for us. We may, however, identify with many ingroups. When we interact with another person, we categorize that person into an ingroup or an outgroup. We experience more uncertainty and anxiety when we communicate with members of outgroups than when we communicate with members of ingroups.

There are numerous other factors that affect the amount of uncertainty and anxiety we experience in a particular situation. The degree to which we are familiar with the situation and know how to behave, the expectations we have for our own and others' behavior, and the degree to which we perceive ourselves to be similar to the other person, for example, influence our level of uncertainty and anxiety.[12] Our ability to reduce our uncertainty and anxiety, in turn, influence the degree to which we can communicate effectively.

I do not mean to imply that we totally want to reduce our uncertainty and anxiety when we communicate with strangers. Low levels of uncertainty and anxiety are not functional. If anxiety is too low, we do not care enough to perform well. If uncertainty is too low, we get bored. Moderate levels of uncertainty and anxiety are desirable for effectiveness and adaptation.[13]

ASSESSING YOUR UNCERTAINTY AND ANXIETY

Table 1.1 contains two short questionnaires designed to help you assess the amount of general uncertainty and anxiety you experience when you interact with strangers. Take a couple of minutes to complete the questionnaires now.

The scores on the two questionnaires range from 5 to 25. The higher your scores, the more uncertainty and anxiety you experience when you interact with strangers. I will not present "average" scores on these questionnaires (or any others presented in the book). Average scores will not help you to understand your own communication behavior. What will help is recognizing that the higher your score, the more likely you are to have instances of ineffective communication when you interact with strangers. Throughout the remainder of the book, I point out things you can do to reduce your uncertainty and anxiety when communicating with strangers.

Table 1.1 Assessing Your Intergroup Uncertainty and Anxiety

The purpose of these two short questionnaires is to help you assess the amount of uncertainty and anxiety you experience when you communicate with strangers. Respond to each statement by indicating the degree to which the adjectives are applicable when you interact with strangers. If you "Never" have the experience, answer 1 in the space provided; if you "Almost Never" have the experience, answer 2; if you "Sometimes" have the experiences and sometimes do not, answer 3; if you "Almost Always" have the experience, answer 4; if you "Always" have the experience, answer 5.

Anxiety

When I interact with strangers, I am
_____ 1. anxious
_____ 2. frustrated
_____ 3. under stress
_____ 4. insecure
_____ 5. concerned

Uncertainty

When I interact with strangers, I am
_____ 1. not confident
_____ 2. uncertain how to behave
_____ 3. indecisive
_____ 4. not able to predict their behavior
_____ 5. not able to understand them

To find your scores, add the numbers you wrote next to each of the items. Construct separate scores for anxiety and uncertainty. Scores range from 5 to 25. The higher your score, the more anxiety and uncertainty you experience when interacting with strangers.

SOURCE: These questionnaires are adapted from Stephan and Stephan (1985).
NOTE: I draw a distinction between uncertainty and anxiety which Stephan and Stephan do not. This is necessary to be consistent with the theory on which the book is based.

The questionnaires in Table 1.1 are designed to assess the "generalized" uncertainty and anxiety you experience when interacting with strangers. You can also use them to assess your uncertainty and anxiety when communicating with members of a specific group or even a specific individual who is different. To do this, substitute "When interacting with (name of group or individual)" for "When I interact with strangers" in the questionnaires.

❏ Communicative Predictions

To reduce uncertainty and anxiety when we communicate, we make predictions about others' behavior. In Gerald Miller and Mark Steinberg's (1975) words, "when people communicate they make predictions about the effects, or outcomes, of their communication behaviors; that is, they choose among various communicative strategies on the basis of predictions about how the person receiving the message will respond" (p. 7; italics omitted).

THE PREDICTION-MAKING PROCESS

Sometimes we are very conscious of the predictions we make and sometimes we are not highly aware of them. When we meet someone whom we find attractive and whom we want to see again, for example, we may think of alternative ways to arrange a next meeting or date, and then select the strategy we think will work best. Under conditions like this, we are aware of the predictions we make.

When we meet someone we know for the first time in a day, we might say "Hi. How are you?". While we are not highly aware of it, we are making an implicit prediction; namely, that the other person will respond something like "Hi. I'm fine and you?". Assuming the other person responds in this way, we would not be highly aware of having made a prediction. If, in contrast, the other person says, "Hi. I'm horrible. I've really been feeling bad today," we would have to stop and think about what to say because our implicit prediction was not confirmed. The degree to which we are conscious of our communication, therefore, depends on the circumstances in which we find ourselves and the responses we receive from others.

When we communicate with others, we try to develop explanations for their behavior so we can understand why they communicate with us the way they do. Our explanations for why people behave the way they do affect the predictions we make. If in the above example, we assume that our acquaintance is feeling bad because he or she is physically ill, we will respond in one way. If we assume, in contrast, that she or he is feeling bad because of some emotional reason, we will react differently.

Situational and dispositional factors influence the predictions we make and the explanations we construct. Situational factors include the characteristics of the setting in which we are communicating; for example, the time, place, physical setting, the number of people involved, characteristics of the people involved, and so forth. Individuals, of course, attach different meanings to these factors. Dispositional factors are internal to the individuals involved. They include past experiences and expectations that predispose individuals to perceive certain behavior and interpret them in selected ways.

LEVELS OF DATA

Miller and Steinberg contend that we use three different types of "data" in making predictions about others: "cultural," "sociological," and "psychological." People in any culture generally behave in a regular way because of the norms, rules, and values of their culture. This regularity allows cultural information to be used in making predictions. Gerald Miller and Michael Sunnafrank (1982) point out that "knowledge about another person's culture—its language, beliefs, and prevailing ideology—often permits predictions of the person's probable response to messages. . . . Upon first encountering . . . [another person], cultural information provides the only grounds for communicative predictions" (p. 226). If we are introduced to a person from the United States,[14] we can make certain assumptions about the person understanding introduction rituals. We implicitly predict, for example, that if we stick out our right hand to shake hands, she or he will do the same.

Our predictions are based on the category in which we place the other person (e.g., member of my culture, not member of my culture). One of the major cognitive tools we use to define ourselves in terms of the world in which we live is social categorization. Social categorization refers to the way we order our social environment (i.e., the people with whom we come in contact) by grouping people in a way that makes sense to us (Tajfel, 1978). We may, for example, divide people into women and men, white and nonwhite, black and nonblack, "Americans" and foreigners, to name only a few of the sets of categories we use. In categorizing others and ourselves, we become aware of being members of social groups. A social group can be thought of as two or more people who define themselves as sharing a common bond (J. C. Turner, 1982).

Once we place someone in a social category, our stereotype of people in that category is activated. Stereotypes are the mental pictures we have of a group of people. Our stereotypes create expectations about how people from our own and other cultures/ethnic groups will behave. They may be accurate or inaccurate and others may fulfill our expectations or violate them. When we travel to another culture or interact with people from another culture, we cannot base our predictions of their behavior on our cultural rules and norms. This inevitably will lead to misunderstanding. If we want to communicate effectively, we must use our knowledge of the other culture to make predictions. If we have little or no knowledge of the other culture, we have no basis for making predictions. "This fact explains the uneasiness and perceived lack of control most people experience when thrust into an alien culture; they not only lack information about the individuals with whom they must communicate, they are bereft of information concerning shared cultural norms and values" (Miller & Sunnafrank, 1982, p. 227).

Sociological predictions are based on memberships in or aspirations to particular social groups or social roles. Miller and Sunnafrank argue that sociological data are the principal kind used to predict behavior of people from our culture. Group memberships based on ethnicity, gender, religion, disabilities, gender orientation, and so forth, are used to predict others' behavior. Roles such as professor, physician, clerk, supervisor, and so forth, also provide a basis for the sociological predictions we make.

When we base our predictions on cultural or sociological information, we are assuming that the people within the category (e.g., the culture or ethnic group) are similar. While individuals within a category share similarities (e.g., there are similarities people born and raised in the United States share), individuals within each of the categories also differ. When we are able to discriminate how individuals are similar to and different from other members of the same category, we are using psychological data to make predictions. The use of psychological data involves taking the specific person with whom we are communicating and how she or he will respond to our messages into consideration when we make our predictions.

Miller and Steinberg point out that we rely on cultural and sociological data in the vast majority of the interactions we have. There is nothing "wrong" with this. It is natural and it is necessary to allow us to deal with the complexity of our social environment. Imagine going into a restaurant and having to "get to know" your waiter or waitress so that you could make psychological predictions about his or her behavior before you could place your order. This would complicate our lives and is not necessary. We can communicate effectively with a waitress or waiter without using psychological data. Sociological data are all that are necessary to get our order correct. The same is true for most other role relationships that do not involve extended interaction (e.g., with clerks, mechanics, etc.).

When we communicate frequently with someone in a specific role relationship, using psychological data becomes important. Physicians who treat all patients alike (e.g., use only sociological data) will not be very effective. Successfully treating patients requires knowledge of them both as patients and as individuals (e.g., specific information about the other person and how he or she is similar to and different from other members of her or his groups). Communicating effectively with strangers also requires differentiating individuals from the groups of which they are members. Relying completely on cultural and/or sociological data when communicating with strangers over an extended period of time inevitably leads to misunderstandings. Effective communication requires that some psychological data be used.

❑ Social Categorization and Communication

Miller and Steinberg argue that we should limit the use of the term "interpersonal communication" to those encounters in which most of the predictions we make about others are based on psychological data. They contend that when most of our predictions about another person are based on cultural or sociological data (using social categorizations) we are engaging in "noninterpersonal communication." Another way of thinking about this is to say that we are engaging in "intergroup" communication. The distinction between these two "types" of communication is important and deserves further discussion. To explain the differences it is necessary to talk about the self-concept or how we define ourselves.

Our self-concept, how we define ourselves, consists of two components—our personal identity and our social identity.[15] Our personal identity includes those aspects of our self-definition that make us unique individuals. I may, for example, see myself as a caring person who wants to improve relations between people from different groups. Our personal identities are derived from our unique individual experiences. Our social identities, in contrast, are derived from our shared memberships in social groups.[16]

Our communication behavior can be based on our personal and/or our social identities. In a particular situation, we may choose (either consciously or unconsciously) to define ourselves communicatively as unique persons or as members of groups. When our communication behavior is based mostly on our personal identities, interpersonal communication can be said to take place. When we define ourselves mostly in terms of our social identities (including our cultural and ethnic identities), in contrast, intergroup communication can be said to occur.

Henri Tajfel and John Turner (1979) believe that behavior can vary from being "purely intergroup" to "purely interpersonal." They contend that pure intergroup communication can take place. An air force bomber crew that does not draw any distinctions among the people on whom they are dropping bombs (i.e., they see them all as the "enemy") is one example of pure intergroup communication. If the members of the bomber crew start drawing distinctions among the people on whom they are dropping bombs (e.g., recognizing that some of them are children), they would no longer be engaged in pure intergroup communication.

Pure interpersonal communication, in contrast, cannot occur, according to Tajfel and Turner. They argue, and I concur, that group memberships influence even the most intimate forms of communication. Consider the communication between two lovers. While it might seem that group memberships and social identities would not influence this form of communication, they do. Whether we define ourselves as heterosexual, homosexual, or bisexual (part of our social identities), for example, influences the gender of the partners we select and the way we communicate with them.

Thinking of interpersonal and intergroup communication as varying along a continuum or being a dichotomy oversimplifies the nature of the communication process. In actuality, our personal *and* social identities influence all of our communication behavior, even though one may predominate in a particular situation. When our social identities have a greater influence on our behavior than our personal identities, however, there is an increased chance of misunderstandings occurring because we are likely to interpret others' behavior based on our group memberships.

In order to overcome the potential for misunderstandings that can occur when our social identities predominate, we must recognize that we share a common identity with strangers (i.e., we are all humans). At the same time, we must acknowledge our differences and try to understand them and how they influence our communication.[17] The remainder of the book is devoted to presenting information and skills that can be used to increase the accuracy of our interpretations of members' of other groups behavior. In the next chapter, I examine effective communication in more detail.

2

Effective Communication with Strangers

In the previous chapter, I discussed the process of communication, isolated two functions of communication (uncertainty and anxiety reduction), and differentiated interpersonal and intergroup communication. In this chapter, I extend the discussion of the nature of communication by defining effective communication and overviewing how cultural and ethnic factors influence our interpretations of others' messages. I also examine the relationship between consciousness and communication.

❑ Effective and Ineffective Communication

In the movie *Cool Hand Luke*, Paul Newman plays Luke, a man put in prison for destroying a parking meter. While in prison, Luke constantly gets into trouble with the prison staff. At one point when Luke had not done something that the Warden asked him to do, the Warden says to Luke, "What we have here is a failure to communicate." On the surface, the Warden's statement makes sense. It is, however, incomplete. The Warden and Luke communicated, but they did not communicate effectively.

> *Communication is effective to the extent that we can minimize misunderstandings.*

EFFECTIVE COMMUNICATION DEFINED

To say we communicated does not imply an outcome. Communication is a process involving the exchange of messages and the creation of meaning. As indicated in the previous chapter, no two people ever attach the same meaning to a message. Whether or not a specific instance of communication is effective or not depends on the degree to which the participants attach similar meanings to the messages exchanged. Stated differently, communication is effective to the extent that we are able to minimize misunderstandings. "To say that meaning in communication is never totally the same for all communicators is not to say that communication is impossible or even difficult—only that it is imperfect" (Fisher, 1978, p. 257).

When we communicate, we attach meaning to (or interpret) messages we construct and transmit to others. We also attach meaning to (or interpret) messages we receive from others. We are not always aware of this process, but we do it nevertheless. To say that two people communicated effectively requires that the two attach relatively similar meanings to the messages sent and received (e.g., they interpret the messages similarly). William Powers and David Lowrey (1984) refer to this as "basic communication fidelity"—"the degree of congruence between the cognitions [or thoughts] of two or more individuals following a communication event" (p. 58).

Harry Triandis (1977) argues that effectiveness involves making "isomorphic attributions" (isomorphic implies being similar; attributions involve assigning a quality or characteristic to something). Everett Rogers and Lawrence Kincaid (1981) take a slightly different position. They suggest that "mutual understanding" is the goal of communication. Mutual understanding is the extent to which one person's estimate of the meaning another person attaches to a message actually matches the meaning the other person attaches to a message.[1]

Mutual understanding does not mean there is agreement. It is possible for us to have mutual understanding and either agree or disagree with each other. We also could have mutual misunderstanding and either agree or disagree. An illustration should clarify the difference. Assume for the moment that we are trying to decide on what movie to see tonight. I want to see Movie X and do not want to see Movie Y. You want to see Movie Y and do not want to see Movie X. We each state our positions and the other person's position is clear. In this situation, we have mutual understanding, but we disagree. If I had not stated my position clearly and I led you to believe that I want to see Movie X, but really wanted to see Movie Y, we would have mutual misunderstanding, but actually agree.

Misunderstandings can occur for a variety of reasons when we communicate with strangers. We may not encode our message in a way that it can be understood by others, strangers may misinterpret what we say, or both can occur simultaneously. The "problems" that occur may be due to our or a stranger's pronunciation, grammar, familiarity with the topic being discussed, familiarity with the other person, familiarity with the other person's native language, fluency in the other person's language, and/or social factors (Gass & Varonis, 1984). If we are familiar with and/or fluent in the other person's language, for example, we can usually understand them better when they speak our language than if we know nothing about their language.

Generally speaking, the greater our cultural and linguistic knowledge, and the more our beliefs overlap with the strangers with whom we communicate, the less the likelihood there will be misunderstandings. Lack of linguistic and cultural knowledge contributes to misunderstandings because we "listen to speech, form a hypothesis about what routine is being enacted, and then rely on social background knowledge and co-occurance expectations to evaluate what is intended and what attitudes are conveyed" (Gumperz, 1982, p. 171).

SCRIPTED COMMUNICATION

We are not always aware of making decisions about the routines we enact. As indicated in Chapter 1, much of our communication behavior is habitual. When we are communicating habitually, we are following scripts—"a coherent sequence of events expected by the individual involving him [or her] either as a participant or an observer" (Abelson, 1976, p. 33). According to Ellen Langer (1978), when we first encounter a new situation, we consciously seek cues to guide our behavior. As we have repeated experiences with the same event, we have less need to consciously think about our behavior. "The more often we engage in the activity, the more likely it is that we rely on scripts for the completion of the activity and the less likely there will be any correspondence between our actions and those thoughts of ours that occur simultaneously" (Langer, 1978, p. 39).

Much of our behavior is habitual or based on scripts we have learned. The distance we stand from each other, for example, is based on the rewards and punishments we received while being socialized as members of our culture. When we are engaging in habitual or scripted behavior, we are not highly aware of what we are doing or saying. To borrow an analogy from flying a plane, we are on "automatic pilot." In Langer's (1978) terminology, we are "mindless." Recent research, however, suggests that we do not communicate totally on automatic pilot. Rather, we pay sufficient attention so that we can recall key words in the conversations we have (Kitayama & Burnstein, 1988).

When we communicate on automatic pilot, we interpret incoming messages based on the symbolic systems we learned as children. A large part of this system is shared with other members of our culture, our ethnic group, our religion, and our family, to name only a few of our group memberships. A part of our symbolic system, however, is unique and based on specific life experiences. No two people share the same symbolic system.

Much of our habitual or scripted behavior involves superficial interactions with other members of our culture or ethnic group in which we rely mainly on cultural or sociological data. The meanings we attach to specific messages and the meanings others attach to these messages are relatively similar. This is due, in part, to the fact that the scripts we enact provide us with shared interpretations of our behavior. While there are differences in our meanings, the differences are not large enough to make our communication ineffective. Under these conditions, we do not need to consciously think about our communication to be relatively "effective."

SOCIAL CATEGORIES AND SCRIPTS

In addition to following scripts, the categories in which we place people can be a source of our going on automatic pilot. As indicated in the previous chapter, we categorize people into groupings that make sense to us. These categories are often based on physical (e.g., gender, race, etc.) or cultural (e.g., cultural or ethnic background) characteristics, but we also can categorize other in terms of their attitudes or approaches to life:

> We adopt sets of categories which serve as ways of managing phenomena. The most fully developed products of this tendency are ideologies, the systems of ideas that rationalize, justify, and sanctify our lives. Nationalism, communism, existentialism, Christianity, Buddhism—all provide us with identities, rules of action, and interpretations of how and why things happen as they do. (Trungpa, 1973, p. 6)

The categories in which we place others affect our interpretations. Once we place an individual in a category, our

stereotype of people in that category influences the predictions we make and how we interpret his or her behavior. Basing our predictions on categories usually
leads to what Langer calls "mindless" behavior. That is, we rely on our expectations
of people in that category to guide our
behavior and interpretations and we are
not conscious of our communication behavior. While categorical information is
useful in making predictions, people can
be placed into many different categories.
When I interact with a student in one of
my classes off campus, I do not use student
as the main category on which to base my
predictions. The student's social identity as a student, however,
may be the one guiding his or her behavior. To communicate
effectively, we have to negotiate the identities we are going to
use in the conversation.

*Misunderstand-
ings result from
our interpreta-
tions of others'
behavior, not
their behavior
per se.*

MISINTERPRETATIONS OF MESSAGES

When we are communicating with strangers and basing our
interpretations on our symbolic systems, ineffective communication usually occurs. Consider a white teacher interacting with
a black student raised in the lower class subculture. The teacher
asks the student a question. In answering the question, the
student does not look the teacher in the eyes. The teacher, in all
likelihood, would interpret the student's behavior as disrespectful and/or assume that the student is hiding something.
Establishing eye contact is expected in the white, middle-class
subculture in the United States when you are telling the truth
and being respectful. The student's intent, on the other hand,
may have been to show respect to the teacher given that children in the lower class black subculture in the United States
are taught not to make eye contact with people they respect.
Situations like this lead to misunderstanding and ineffective
communication.

To further illustrate the misunderstandings that can occur when we communicate with strangers, consider the following example presented by Harry Triandis (1975, pp. 42-43). The example is drawn from the files of his colleague George Vassiliou, a Greek psychiatrist, and it involves a segment of interaction between a supervisor from the United States and a subordinate from Greece. In the segment, the supervisor wants the employee to participate in decisions (a norm in the United States), while the subordinate expects to be told what to do (a norm in Greece):

Behavior		*Attribution*	
AMERICAN:	How long will it take you to finish this report?	AMERICAN:	I asked him to participate.
		GREEK:	His behavior makes no sense. He is the boss. Why doesn't he tell me?
GREEK:	I do not know. How long should it take?	AMERICAN:	He refuses to take responsibility.
		GREEK:	I asked him for an order.
AMERICAN:	You are in the best position to analyze time requirements.	AMERICAN:	I press him to take responsibility for his own actions.
		GREEK:	What nonsense! I better give him an answer.
GREEK:	10 days.	AMERICAN:	He lacks the ability to estimate time; this estimate is totally inadequate.
AMERICAN:	Take 15. It is agreed you will do it in 15 days?	AMERICAN:	I offer a contract.

GREEK:	These are my orders. 15 days.

In fact the report needed 30 days of regular work. So the Greek worked day and night, but at the end of the 15th day, he still needed one more day's work.

AMERICAN:	Where is my report?	AMERICAN:	I am making sure he fulfills his contract.
		GREEK:	He is asking for the report.
GREEK:	It will be ready tomorrow.	(Both attribute that it is not ready.)
AMERICAN:	But we agreed that it would be ready today.	AMERICAN:	I must teach him to fulfill a contract.
		GREEK:	The stupid, incompetent boss! Not only did he give me wrong orders, but he does not appreciate that I did a 30-day job in 16 days.

The Greek hands in his resignation.		The American is surprised.	
		GREEK:	I can't work for such a man.

As these two examples illustrate, our culture and ethnicity influence the attributions we make about others' behavior. The unique aspects of our symbolic systems also can be problematic when we are communicating with people we know reasonably well. In fact, it appears that we have more misunderstandings with people we know well than with people we do not know well.[2] One reason for this is that we *assume* that people we know well have meanings that are similar to ours. Because the topics of conversations we hold with people we know (including co-workers) are often more important than those we hold with people we do not know well, small differences in meanings attached to messages may lead to misunderstandings.

NEED FOR COGNITIVE CONTROL OF
UNCONSCIOUS INTERPRETATIONS

It is important to recognize that the misunderstandings that we have with others are the result of our interpretations of their behavior, not their behavior per se.[3] I may say, for example, "You make me angry." This is not an accurate statement. While it is true I would not have experienced anger if you had not behaved in a certain way, my anger is based on how I interpreted your behavior, not your actual behavior.

Consider the following example. If I arrange to meet my friend Charles at 6:00 P.M. and he does not arrive until 6:30 P.M., I may be upset with Charles. The reason I am upset is based on my interpretation of what "being on time" means and assuming that it means the same thing for Charles. For Charles, arriving within a half hour of the time on which we agreed may be "on time." For me to communicate effectively with Charles, it is important that I understand that my being upset is due to my interpretation of his behavior, not his actual behavior, and that his interpretation of his behavior may be different than mine.

To decrease the chance of misinterpretations of others' messages based on our unconscious interpretations, we must be aware of our "normal" tendencies. Aaron Beck (1988) outlines five principles of cognitive therapy that are useful in understanding how misinterpretations occur:

(1) We can never know the state of mind—the attitudes, thoughts, and feelings—of other people.

(2) We depend on signals, which are frequently ambiguous, to inform us about the attitudes and wishes of other people.

(3) We use our own coding system, which may be defective, to decipher these signals.

(4) Depending on our own state of mind at a particular time, we may be biased in our method of interpreting other people's behavior, that is, how we decode.

(5) The degree to which we believe that we are correct in divining another person's motives and attitudes is not related to the actual accuracy of our belief. (p. 18)

Cognitive therapy focuses on how individuals interpret and misinterpret others' behavior. Many of the techniques used are valuable in improving our ability to communicate effectively and will be incorporated in the remainder of the book.

❏ Mindfulness

Cognitive therapists stress that we must become aware of our communication behavior in order to correct our tendency to misinterpret others' behavior and communicate more effectively. Social psychologists refer to this as becoming "mindful" of our behavior.

THE NATURE OF MINDFULNESS

Ellen Langer (1989) isolates three qualities of mindfulness: "(1) creation of new categories; (2) openness to new information; and (3) awareness of more than one perspective" (p. 62). She points out that "categorizing is a fundamental and natural human activity. It is the way we come to know the world. Any attempt to eliminate bias by attempting to eliminate the perception of differences is doomed to failure" (p. 154).[4]

Langer argues that what we need to do is learn to make more, not fewer, distinctions. To illustrate, Langer uses an example of people who are in the category "cripple." If we see all people in this category as the same, we start treating the category in which we place a person as his or her identity. If we draw additional distinctions within this category (e.g., create new categories), on the other hand, it stops us from treating the person as a category. If we see a person with a "lame leg," we do not necessarily treat her or him as a "cripple."

Openness to new information and awareness of more than one perspective are related to focusing on the process, rather than the outcome. Langer argues that

an outcome orientation in social situations can induce mindless-
ness. If we think we know how to handle a situation, we don't feel
a need to pay attention. If we respond to the situation as very
familiar (as a result, for example, of overlearning), we notice only
minimal cues necessary to carry out the proper scenarios. If, on
the other hand, the situation is strange, we might be so preoccu-
pied with the thought of failure ("what if I make a fool of myself?")
that we miss nuances of our own and others' behavior. In this
sense, we are mindless with respect to the immediate situation,
although we may be thinking quite actively about outcome related
issues. (p. 34)

Langer believes that focusing on the process (e.g., how we do
something) forces us to be mindful of our behavior and pay
attention to the situations in which we find ourselves. It is only
when we are mindful of the process of our communication that
we can determine how our interpretations of messages differ
from others' interpretations of those messages.

CONDITIONS PROMOTING MINDFULNESS

Sometimes we become mindful of our communication without any effort on our part because of the circumstances in
which we find ourselves. We tend to engage in habitual behavior and follow scripts only when they are available and
nothing unusual to the scripts is encountered. There are, however, several factors that will cause us to become mindful of
our communication: "(1) in novel situations where, by definition, no appropriate script exists, (2) where external factors
prevent completion of a script, (3) when scripted behavior
becomes effortful because substantially more of the behavior
is required than is usual, (4) when a discrepant outcome is
experienced, or (5) where multiple scripts come into conflict"
(Berger & Douglas, 1982, pp. 46-47).

We often are mindful of our behavior when we communicate
with strangers because they may act in a deviant or unexpected
fashion or we do not have a script to guide our communication
with them. The "problem" is that we usually are mindful of the
outcome, not the process.

Because we tend to interpret others' behavior based on our own frame of reference, to communicate effectively with strangers we need to become mindful of our process of communication, even when we are engaging in habitual behavior. I am not suggesting that we try to be mindful at all times. This would be impossible. Rather, I am suggesting that when we know there is a high potential for misunderstanding, we need to be mindful and consciously aware of the process of communication that is taking place.

If we are mindful of our communication with strangers from a specific group over time, eventually we should become unconsciously competent in communicating with people from this group. Given that the knowledge necessary to make accurate predictions of strangers' behavior is culture or ethnic group specific, our unconscious competence may not generalize to our communication with strangers from other groups. The general skills (e.g., recognizing when misunderstandings occur) we have learned, however, should "trigger" us to become mindful when needed.

❑ Improving Communication Effectiveness

When we become mindful, there are several things we can do to improve our communication effectiveness. We can, for example, "negotiate meanings" with the other person. Negotiating meanings involves seeking clarification of meanings in the middle of a conversation when we realize a misunderstanding has occurred (Varonis & Gass, 1985). This appears to be the most widely used technique to deal with misunderstandings. Attempts to negotiate meanings usually are initiated by the person whose native language is being spoken.

Another technique we can use is "repairs." Repairs involve asking the other person to repeat what was said when we do not understand (Gass & Varonis, 1985). Repair sequences usually are initiated by the person speaking in his or her second language. Research suggests that repairs are a necessary part of conversations when one person is speaking a second language (Schwartz, 1980).

While communication competency is discussed in detail in Chapter 6, I devote the remainder of this chapter to presenting four "skills" that are necessary to negotiate meanings and make repairs in conversations with strangers, as well as members of our ingroups: (1) separating descriptions, interpretations, and evaluations of behavior; (2) using feedback; (3) listening effectively, and (4) metacommunicating.

SEPARATING DESCRIPTION, INTERPRETATION,
AND EVALUATION

When we communicate with others we do not describe their behavior. Rather, when we decode incoming messages, we immediately interpret those messages. Because we tend to use our own symbolic system to interpret incoming messages, we often misinterpret messages transmitted by people who are different. In order to understand people who are different, we must become mindful and try to figure out the meaning they attached to the message transmitted to us.[5]

Describing behavior refers to an actual report of what was observed with a minimum of distortion and without attributing meaning to the behavior. Description includes what we see, hear, feel, touch, and taste. In other words, it is information that comes from our sense organs. "He breathed in my face when we talked" and "She did not look me in the eyes when we talked" are both descriptive statements. Neither attaches meaning to the behavior, both only describe the behavior observed.

An interpretation is the meaning or social significance attached to the behavior. It involves what we think about what we observed. There are multiple interpretations for any one description. To illustrate, consider the second description: "She did not look me in the eyes when we talked." What are the possible interpretations of this behavior? To develop a list of possible interpretations we must be mindful. If we respond in a mindless fashion, we will only think about the interpretations used in our subculture. Not looking someone in the eye in the white, middle-class subculture of the United States, for example, usually is interpreted as the person is not telling the truth. Other possible interpretations in this subculture include, but are not limited to, she is shy, she is hiding something, and she is being disrespectful. If, as in the example presented earlier, the person who did not look us in the eye is black, we should also consider the interpretation that she is being respectful.

After we have developed a list of possible interpretations, we must determine the most probable interpretation the other person is placing on the message. If we know the other person, we can rely on psychological data about him or her to make an "educated guess." If we do not know the other person, we must rely on the cultural and/or sociological data we have to make an educated guess. I talk about how we can gather the information we need to make an educated guess when we do not have the necessary data in Chapter 6.

Once we have determined the most probable interpretation, we can then evaluate the behavior. Obviously, we would evaluate the interpretations "she is lying" and "she is showing respect" in the preceding example much differently.

Only by separating descriptions, interpretations, and evaluations of behavior can we understand strangers. If we interpret their behavior without describing it first, we inevitably use our own symbol system to interpret their behavior. This will lead to misinterpretations a large percent of the time.

USING FEEDBACK

We seek feedback from others and provide feedback on their communication when there is uncertainty present (Ashford & Cummings, 1983). Feedback refers to "the response listeners give to others about their behavior. . . . Feedback from others enables us to understand how our behavior affects them, and allows us to modify our behavior to achieve our desired goals" (Haslett & Ogilvie, 1988, p. 385). Feedback may be verbal or nonverbal. Affective or evaluative feedback tends to be given nonverbally, while cognitive or content feedback tends to be given verbally (Zajonc, 1980).

By paying attention to the feedback we receive and using it effectively, we engage in "a series of diminishing mistakes—a dwindling series of under-and-over corrections converging on the goal" (Deutsch, 1968, p. 390). To the extent that we use feedback effectively, we converge toward mutual understanding and shared meanings. If we do not receive feedback and use it effectively, however, we will diverge from shared meanings and misunderstandings will occur.

Beth Haslett and John Ogilvie (1988) provide concrete suggestions for giving effective feedback when communicating with people from the same culture and/or ethnic group. First, feedback should be direct and specific, and be supported by evidence (e.g., a rationale needs to be given). Indirect and vague feedback generally is not effective with people in the United States (especially in the middle-class subculture). Second, the issue on which the feedback is given needs to be separated from the person. Avoid judging the person being given feedback. Third, present the situation on which feedback is being given as a mutual problem (e.g., do not blame the other person for screwing-up). Fourth, do not overload someone with negative feedback; mix negative feedback with positive feedback. Fifth, provide the feedback at a time close to the occurrence, but at a time the other person will be receptive. If I am emotionally upset and unable to control my anger, for example, it will not do any good to give me feedback until I have calmed down. Sixth, deliver feedback in an assertive, dynamic, responsive, and relaxed style. Finally, be trustworthy, fair, credible, and preserve the other person's public image when you give feedback.

These suggestions for providing feedback are based on research with whites in the United States. Modifications are necessary when dealing with strangers. The modifications that are necessary cannot be discussed in detail at this point because I have not discussed culture and ethnicity (the focus of the next chapter). An example, however, can illustrate the necessity of providing feedback that is sensitive to the other person's cultural and/or ethnic background.

Assume that I (a white male from the United States) want to present feedback to a Japanese male friend with whom I am communicating in Japan. If I am direct in the feedback that I give my friend, he may perceive my feedback as a threat to his public image. The reason for this is that Japanese try to preserve harmony in relations with friends. To accomplish this, they use an indirect style of communication. If I am direct and he perceives this as a threat, my feedback will be ineffective. To provide culturally sensitive feedback, I have to be indirect in the way I give it. If we are in the United States speaking English, I can be more direct than if we are in Japan speaking Japanese. Knowing when and how to modify our feedback is an issue of communication competence.

LISTENING EFFECTIVELY

Carol Roach and Nancy Wyatt (1988) point out that listening is not a natural activity, it is not a passive activity as most of us assume, and most of us are not very skilled listeners. Hearing is a natural, automatic process, while listening is the "process of discriminating and identifying which sounds are meaningful or important to us and which aren't" (p. 2). Successful listening, therefore, is a purposive activity (i.e., it requires that we are mindful). More specifically, "real listening involves taking in new information and checking it against what you already know, selecting important ideas from unimportant ideas, searching for categories to store the information in (or creating categories), and predicting what's coming next in order to be ready for it" (p. 4). Most of us need practice to accomplish this.

Many writers suggest that we engage in "active" or "empathic" listening.[6] Carl Rogers (1980), for example, believes we should enter "the private perceptual world of the other and becoming thoroughly at home in it. It involves being sensitive, moment by moment, to the changing felt needs which flow in this other person" (p. 142).

John Stewart and Milt Thomas (1990) point out that active and empathic listening focus on the other person and not what is going on between the people communicating.[7] Stewart and Thomas suggest "dialogic listening" as an alternative.[8] Their notion of dialogic listening involves focusing on the process of communication that is occurring between the communicators at the time they are communicating. They believe we should focus on the meanings that are being created, rather than only trying to understand the other person or get our ideas across (an idea similar to Langer's notion of focusing on the process and not the outcome when being mindful). This requires that we listen without presupposing any particular outcome. It also requires that we focus on what is being said and how it is being said in the conversation we are having. Stated differently, we must stop the "internal monologue" (e.g., thinking about what we are going to say next) that is going on in our heads (Howell, 1982).

Dialogic listening is a way to "develop ideas and suggestions, tease out nuances, and help define incomplete ideas" (Stewart & Thomas, 1990, p. 202). One of the behaviors we can use to accomplish this is to ask others to "say more" when we are unsure of what they mean. Another important behavior is paraphrasing—summarizing what another person said in our own words. Stewart and Thomas contend that ideally we should go a step further. "If you're paraphrasing for fidelity and correspondence, you're satisfied and 'finished' with the task as soon as you've successfully reproduced 'what she means.' . . . We're suggesting that you go beyond correspondence to creativity" (p. 205). Paraphrasing is a two-way street. If we think another person does not understand us, we should ask him or her to paraphrase what we say. This, however, is not something we usually do when we communicate and it takes practice.

Dialogic listening obviously lengthens the amount of time it will take to have a conversation. There are other potential "problems" with the approach that stem from the fact that it is not the way we "normally" listen. Because most people do not practice dialogic listening, they may wonder what is happening when we ask them to "say more" or paraphrase what we said. Whether or not they cooperate will have a lot to do with our attitude. If we demonstrate that we really want to understand them and are not just playing some game, it will increase the likelihood they will cooperate.

METACOMMUNICATING

The final general skill necessary for effective communication is metacommunicating. Metacommunicating is communicating about our communication (Watzlawick, Beavin, & Jackson, 1967). The way we say what we say (i.e., the relational aspect of the message), for example, is a form of metacommunication because it tells the other person how we feel about them. This is, however, an implicit form of metacommunication. Implicit metacommunication is a part of all of the messages we send to others. The implicit metacommunicative message is transmitted through our tone of voice and nonverbal behaviors. When we are communicating with strangers implicit metacommunicative messages may lead to misunderstandings because people from other cultures or ethnic backgrounds may interpret our tone of voice or nonverbal behavior differently than we intended.

In order to make sure that our messages are being interpreted as we meant them to be and that we are interpreting others' messages as they intended, we must sometimes metacommunicate explicitly. Explicit metacommunication can take many forms. We are metacommunicating explicitly when we tell another person how we interpreted what she or he just said or ask how he or she interpreted our message. Virginia Satir (1967) provides several other examples of explicit metacommunication, including (1) telling the other person what kind of message we are sending and how serious we are about the content; (2) telling the other person why we sent the message we did by referring to our perception of what they want, or the type of response we want; or (3) telling the other person what we want them to do.

No matter what form the explicit metacommunication takes, the goal should be to clarify the meanings we attach to messages. When there are overtly recognizable differences, metacommunication often occurs naturally. When the differences are covert, however, we may not recognize the need to metacommunicate. It is important, therefore, to look out for small signs that misunderstandings have occurred (e.g., puzzled looks, responses not directly related to our messages). These signs are possible indications that metacommunication may be necessary to make sure we are communicating effectively. Like active listening, metacommunication is not something most of us do in our everyday communication with others. It is, nevertheless, necessary to communicate effectively, especially when we are communicating with strangers.

The conceptualization of effective communication and the "skills" I presented in this chapter are applicable to all of our communication. In the remainder of the book, I focus on issues that need special "attention" when we communicate with strangers. Before discussing these issues, however, it is necessary to understand how strangers can differ from us. The next chapter, therefore, is devoted to understanding the nature of cultural and ethnic diversity.

3

Understanding Diversity

In this chapter, I examine the various sources of diversity that influence the way we communicate. Because the focus of the book is on national cultures and ethnic subcultures, I examine them in the most detail. There are, however, several other sources of diversity that affect our communication every day. I, therefore, also discuss gender, disability, religion, age, and gender orientation as social categorizations that affect our communication.

❏ Culture

There is no agreement among social scientists on how to define culture. Culture can be seen as including everything that is human made (e.g., Herskovits, 1955) or as a system of shared meanings (e.g., Geertz, 1973), to name only two possible conceptualizations. Culture also has been equated with communication. Edward T. Hall (1959), for example, believes that "culture is communication and communication is culture" (p. 169).

Clifford Geertz (1966) uses the octopus as a metaphor for culture:

> The problem of cultural analysis is as much a matter of determining independencies as interconnections, gulfs as well as bridges. The appropriate image, if one must have images, of cultural organization, is neither the spider web nor the pile of sand. It is rather more the octopus, whose tentacles are in large part separately integrated, neurally quite poorly connected with one another and with what in the octopus passes for a brain and yet who nonetheless manages to get around and to preserve himself [or herself], for a while anyway, as a viable, if somewhat ungainly entity. (pp. 66-67)

The octopus is an interesting metaphor for culture, but it does not define it sufficiently for us to use the concept to understand our communication with strangers.

While there are many definitions of culture, it is necessary to select one to guide our analysis. I use Roger Keesing's (1974) definition. His definition is long, but not overly technical:

> Culture, conceived as a system of competence shared in its broad design and deeper principles, and varying between individuals in its specificities, is then not all of what an individual knows and thinks and feels about his [or her] world. It is his [or her] theory of what his [or her] fellows know, believe, and mean, his [or her] theory of the code being followed, the game being played, in the society into which he [or she] was born. . . . It is this theory to which a native actor refers in interpreting the unfamiliar or the ambiguous, in interacting with strangers (or supernaturals), and in other settings peripheral to the familiarity of mundane everyday life space; and with which he [or she] creates the stage on which the games of life are played. . . . But note that the actor's "theory" of his [or her] culture, like his [or her] theory of his [or her] language may be in large measure unconscious. Actors follow rules of which they are not consciously aware, and assume

a world to be "out there" that they have in fact created with culturally shaped and shaded patterns of mind. We can recognize that not every individual shares precisely the same theory of the cultural code, that not every individual knows all the sectors of the culture . . . even though no one native actor knows all the culture, and each has a variant version of the code. Culture in this view is ordered not simply as a collection of symbols fitted together by the analyst but as a system of knowledge, shaped and constrained by the way the human brain acquires, organizes, and processes information and creates "internal models of reality." (p. 89)

I use the term culture to refer to the "system of knowledge" that is shared by a large group of people. The "borders" between cultures usually, but not always, coincide with political boundaries between countries. To illustrate, we can speak of the culture of the United States, the Japanese culture, and the Mexican culture. In some countries, however, there is more than one culture.[1] Consider Canada as an example. There is the Anglophone (i.e., English speaking) culture derived from England and there is the Francophone culture derived from France.

Throughout the remainder of the book, I will discuss how culture influences the way we communicate. While I focus on the influence of culture on our communication, I do *not* mean to imply that this is a one-way process. Our communication with other members of our culture can and does influence the form our culture takes. Cultural change, however, takes place over long periods of time. At any given point in time, our communication is influenced more by our culture than we are influencing our culture by our communication.

When I refer to subdivisions of a "national" culture, I use the term subculture. Subculture implies that the group shares some of the larger national culture, but has some values or customs that differ from the larger culture. We can speak of ethnic subcultures (ethnicity is discussed later in this chapter), or an "artistic" subculture, to name only two possibilities. While the focus of this book is on communicating with people from different national cultures and ethnic subcultures, everything said applies to other subcultures as well.

❏ How Cultures Differ

In order to understand similarities and differences in communication across cultures, it is necessary to have a way of
talking about how cultures differ. It does not make any sense
to say that "Jiro communicates indirectly because he is a
Japanese" or that "Adrian communicates directly because he
is from the United States." This does not tell us why there are
differences between the way people communicate in the United
States and Japan. There has to be some aspect of the cultures in
Japan and the United States that are different and this difference, in turn, explains why Japanese communicate indirectly
and people from the United States communicate directly. In
other words, there are variables on which cultures can be different or similar that can be used to explain communication
across cultures. I will refer to these variables as "dimensions of
cultural variability."

There are several different conceptualizations of how cultures differ. It is impossible to discuss them all in a short book
like this. I, therefore, focus on the two that I have found most
useful in understanding similarities and differences in communication across cultures: individualism-collectivism and low-
and high-context communication.[2]

INDIVIDUALISM-COLLECTIVISM

Individualism-collectivism is the major dimension of cultural variability used to explain cross-cultural differences in
behavior.[3] Emphasis is placed on individuals' goals in individualistic cultures, while group goals have precedence over
individuals' goals in collectivistic cultures. Individualistic
cultures, for example, promote "self-realization" for their
members:

> Chief among the virtues claimed by individualist philosophers
> is self-realization. Each person is viewed as having a unique set of
> talents and potentials. The translation of these potentials into

actuality is considered the highest purpose to which one can devote one's life. The striving for self-realization is accompanied by a subjective sense of rightness and personal well-being. (Waterman, 1984, pp. 4-5)

Collectivistic cultures, in contrast, require that individuals fit into the group. This is illustrated by the culture in Kenya:

In Kenyan tribes nobody is an isolated individual. Rather, his [or her] uniqueness is a secondary fact. . . . First, and foremost, he [or she] is several people's contemporary. His [or her] life is founded on these facts economically, socially and physically. In this system group activities are dominant, responsibility is shared and accountability is collective. . . . Because of the emphasis on collectivity, harmony and cooperation among the group tend to be emphasized more than individual function and responsibility. (Saleh & Gufwoli, 1982, p. 327)

In individualistic cultures, "people are supposed to look after themselves and their immediate family only," while in collectivistic cultures, "people belong to ingroups or collectivities which are supposed to look after them in exchange for loyalty" (Hofstede & Bond, 1984, p. 419). The "I" identity has precedence in individualistic cultures over the "we" identity, which takes precedence in collectivistic cultures. The emphasis in individualistic societies is on individuals' initiative and achievement, while emphasis is placed on belonging to groups in collectivistic societies. People in individualistic cultures tend to be universalistic and apply the same value standards to all. People in collectivistic cultures, in contrast, tend to be particularistic and, therefore, apply different value standards for members of their ingroups and outgroups.

Harry Triandis (1988) argues that collectivistic cultures emphasize the goals, needs, and views of the ingroup over those of the individual; the social norms of the ingroup, rather than individual pleasure; shared ingroup beliefs, rather than unique individual beliefs; and a value on cooperation with ingroup members, rather than maximizing individual outcomes. The number of ingroups, the extent of influence for each ingroup, and the depth of the influence must be taken into consideration in the analysis of individualism-collectivism (Triandis, 1988). Because individualistic cultures have many specific ingroups (e.g., family, religion, social clubs, etc.), they exert less influence on individuals than ingroups do in collectivistic cultures, in which there are a few general ingroups (e.g., work group, university, family). While the ingroup may be the same in individualistic and collectivistic cultures, the sphere of its influence is different. The sphere of influence in an individualistic culture is very specific (e.g., the ingroup affects behavior in very specific circumstances), while the sphere of influence in a collectivistic is very general (e.g., the ingroup affects behavior in many different aspects of a person's life).

> *Individualistic and collectivistic tendencies exist in all cultures, but one tends to predominate.*

Ingroups have different rank-orders of importance in collectivistic cultures; some, for example, put family ahead of all other ingroups, while others put their companies ahead of other ingroups (Triandis, 1988). To illustrate, the company often is considered the primary ingroup in Japan (Nakane, 1970), while the family is the primary ingroup in many other collectivistic cultures (e.g., Latin and South America).

INDIVIDUALISTIC AND COLLECTIVISTIC
PERSONALITY ORIENTATIONS

Individualistic and collectivistic tendencies exist in all cultures, but one tends to predominate. Everyone, however, has individualistic and collectivistic thoughts. It is possible, therefore, for there to be collectively oriented persons in an individualistic culture and individualistically oriented persons in collectivistic cultures. Triandis and his associates (1985) call people who have more individualistic than collectivistic thoughts "idiocentrics" and people who have more collectivistic than individualistic thoughts "allocentrics." They found that allocentric tendencies involved three factors: subordinating individual goals to group goals, viewing the ingroup as an extension of the self, and having a strong ingroup identity.

Shalom Schwartz (1990) argues that individualistic and collectivistic values do not necessarily conflict. With respect to individualistic values, he points out that

> hedonism (enjoyment), achievement, self-direction, social power, and stimulation values all serve self interests of the individual, but not necessarily at the expense of any collectivity. . . . These same values might be promoted by leaders or members of collectivities as goals for their ingroup. (p. 143)

With respect to collectivistic tendencies, he indicates that

> prosocial, restrictive conformity, security, and tradition values all focus on promoting the interests of others. It is other people, constituting a collective, who benefit from the actor's concern for them, self-restraint, care for their security, and respect for shared traditions. But this does not necessarily occur at the expense of the actor. (p. 143)

Cultures and individuals, therefore, can have both individualistic and collectivistic tendencies.[4]

ASSESSING YOUR INDIVIDUALISTIC AND
COLLECTIVISTIC TENDENCIES

The two questionnaires in Table 3.1 are designed to help you assess the degree to which you are idiocentric and/or allocentric. Take a few minutes to complete the questionnaires now.

Scores on both questionnaires range from 5 to 25. The higher your score, the more your idiocentric and allocentric tendencies. While one personality orientation probably tends to predominate, you can have high or low scores on both. The important thing to keep in mind is that your tendencies affect your communication with people who have different tendencies.

Table 3.1 Assessing Your Idiocentric and Allocentric Tendencies

The purpose of these two questionnaires is to help you assess your idiocentric and allocentric tendencies. Respond by indicating the degree to which the value reflected in each phrase is important to you: "Opposed to my Values" (answer 1), "Not Important to Me" (answer 2), "Somewhat Important to Me" (answer 3), "Important to Me" (answer 4), or "Very Important to Me" (answer 5).

Idiocentric Tendencies

_____ 1. Obtaining pleasure or sensuous gratification

_____ 2. Being successful by demonstrating my individual competency

_____ 3. Being independent in thought and action

_____ 4. Obtaining status and prestige

_____ 5. Having an exciting and challenging life

Allocentric Tendencies

_____ 1. Preserving and enhancing the welfare of others

_____ 2. Restraining my behavior if it is going to harm others

_____ 3. Safety and stability of people with whom I identify

_____ 4. Harmony in my relations with others

_____ 5. Accepting my cultural and religious traditions

To find your scores, add the numbers you wrote next to each statement. Compute separate scores for your idiocentric and allocentric tendencies. The higher your scores, the more you have these tendencies.

SOURCE: The statements in these questionnaires were adapted from Schwartz (1990).

When we communicate with people from other cultures, we must start from the assumption that they are similar. People from individualistic cultures, for example, assume that people in collectivistic cultures act collectively. This provides valuable information on how to communicate with people from collectivistic cultures. To illustrate, it allows us to predict that people in collectivistic cultures emphasize their social identities over their personal identities when they communicate.[5] To communicate effectively with specific people, however, we must also recognize that not all people in collectivistic cultures are allocentric. In other words, we must be ready to look for individual differences.

LOW- AND HIGH-CONTEXT COMMUNICATION

Individualism-collectivism provides a powerful explanatory framework for understanding cultural similarities and differences in interpersonal communication. Harry Triandis (personal communication, September 4, 1990) points out that

> since in collectivistic cultures relationships with others are extremely important, people learn to pay attention not only to what is said, but also to the context of what is said—the gestures, the orientation of the body, the objects associated with what is being said. In other words they pay more attention to context than people in individualistic cultures. To save face sometimes they let the context speak for itself. For example, in Indonsia a young man courted an upper class woman, and sent his mother to visit the woman's mother to arrange a marriage. The woman's mother served his mother tea and bananas. Since tea is never served with banana that was the signal that the answer is "No." This way the woman's mother did not have to insult his mother by openly saying "No." The objects spoke for her!

Such an incident is not likely to occur in an individualistic culture.

Edward T. Hall (1976) differentiates cultures on the basis of the communication that predominates in the culture. A high-context communication or message is one in which "most of the information is either in the physical context or internalized in the person, while very little is in the coded, explicit, transmitted part of the message" (Hall, 1976, p. 79). A low-context communication or message, in contrast, is one in which "the mass of information is vested in the explicit code" (p. 70). While no culture exists at either end of the continuum, the culture of the United States is placed toward the lower end, slightly above the German, Scandinavian, and Swiss cultures. Most Asian cultures, such as the Japanese, Chinese, and Korean, in contrast, fall toward the high-context end of the continuum.

The level of context influences all other aspects of communication:

> High-context cultures make greater distinction between insiders and outsiders than low-context cultures do. People raised in high-context systems expect more of others than do the participants in low-context systems. When talking about something that they have on their minds, a high-context individual will expect his [or her] interlocutor to know what's bothering him [or her], so that he [or she] doesn't have to be specific. The result is that he [or she] will talk around and around the point, in effect putting all the pieces in place except the crucial one. Placing it properly—this keystone—is the role of his [or her] interlocutor. (Hall, 1976, p. 98)

It appears that low- and high-context communication are the predominant forms of communication in individualistic and collectivistic cultures, respectively.

As suggested above, members of low-context, individualistic cultures tend to communicate in a direct fashion, while members of high-context, collectivistic cultures tend to communicate in an indirect fashion. Donald Levine (1985) describes communication in the Amhara culture in Ethiopia (a collectivistic culture) as follows:

> The Amhara's basic manner of communicating is indirect, often secretive. Amharic conversation abounds with general, evasive remarks, like *Min yeshallal?* ("What is better?") when the speaker has failed to indicate what issue he [or she] is referring to, or *Setagn!* ("Give me!") when the speaker fails to specify what it is he [or she] wants. When the speaker then is quizzed about the issue at hand or the object he [or she] desires, his [or her] reply still may not reveal what is really on his [or her] mind; and if it does, his [or her] interlocutor will likely as not interpret that response as a disguise. (p. 25)

Levine goes on to describe communication in the United States (an individualistic culture) in this way:

> The [North] American way of life, by contrast, affords little room for the cultivation of ambiguity. The dominant [North] American temper calls for clear and direct communication. It expresses itself in such common injunctions as "Say what you mean," "Don't beat around the bush," and "Get to the point." (p. 28)

❏ Ethnicity

Like culture, ethnicity is a "slippery" idea. There are many different definitions of the term. We can, for example, impose ethnic labels on others. When we impose labels on others, however, we may not impose the label the other person would use to describe him- or herself (Barth, 1969). George DeVos (1975) suggests that ethnicity involves the use of some aspect of a group's cultural background to separate themselves from others. Howard Giles and Patricia Johnson (1981), in contrast, see an ethnic group as "those individuals who identify themselves as belonging to the same ethnic category" (p. 202).

In actuality, we can impose an ethnic label on others *and* they identify with an ethnic group. Any time we categorize ourselves as members of a group, we also categorize others as not members of our group and, therefore, members of another group (J. C. Turner, 1987). Categorization of ethnicity may be based on cultural, social, psychological, or biological characteristics (Gorden, 1964).

There have been changes in recent years in the way people in the United States view ethnicity.[6] In the past, an "assimilationist" view of ethnicity predominated and was not questioned. Assimilation refers to the process of giving up one culture and taking on the characteristics of another. Robert Park (1950), for example, argues that the "cycle of contact, competition, accommodation, and eventual assimilation [among ethnic groups] is apparently progressive and unreversibile" (p. 13).[7]

More recently, a "pluralistic" view of ethnicity has predominated. In this view, ethnicity "is an internal attitude which predisposes, but does not make compulsory, the display of ethnic identification in interaction. When it facilitates self-interest, ethnic identity will be made self-evident; it is left latent when it would hinder" (Hraba & Hoiberg, 1983, p. 385). When members of a group decide to exert their ethnicity depends upon the particular circumstances in which they find themselves (Glazer & Moynihan, 1975).

❏ Cultural and Ethnic Identity

Before examining other forms of diversity that influence the way we communicate, we need to briefly discuss our cultural and ethnic identities. As indicated in Chapter 1, our self-concepts consist of our personal and social identities. Our social identities are derived from our memberships in social groups including, but not limited to, our culture, our ethnicity, our gender, our religion, and our age group, to name only a few. The degree to which we identify with these various groups varies from situation to situation. To illustrate, while I am a North American, I do not think about being a member of my culture much in everyday life. When I visit another country, however, my North American identity (my cultural identity) becomes important. I think about being a North American, and my cultural identity plays a large role in influencing my behavior.

THE IMPORTANCE OF CULTURAL AND ETHNIC IDENTITY

While the degree to which we assert our social identities varies from situation to situation, the general degree to which we identify with particular groups appears to remain relatively stable over time. Eugeen Roosens (1989), for example, points out that asserting an ethnic identity helps us define who we are. Specifically, he suggests that our ethnicity offers

> communality in language, a series of customs and symbols, a style, rituals, and appearance, and so forth, which can penetrate life in many ways. These trappings of ethnicity are particularly attractive when one is continually confronted by others who live differently. . . . If I see and experience myself as a member of an ethnic category or group, and others—fellow members and outsiders—recognize me as such, "ways of being" become possible for me that set me apart from the outsiders. These ways of being contribute to the *content* of my self-perceptions. In this sense, I *become* my ethnic allegiance; I experience any attack on the symbols, emblems, or values (cultural elements) that define my ethnicity as an attack on myself. (pp. 17-18)

The language we speak is a major way we mark boundaries between our ethnic group and others.[8] This is true in informal conversations with strangers, acquaintances, and friends, as well as in formal communication situations (e.g., when we talk to our supervisor at work).

Richard Rodriguez (1982) illustrates the importance of language in a description of the effect of hearing his father speak English to an Anglo gas station attendant when he was growing-up:

> I cannot forget the sounds my father made as he spoke. At one point his words slid together to form one word—sounds as confused as the threads of blue and green oil in the puddle next to my shoes. His voice rushed through what he had left to say. And, toward the end, reached falsetto notes, appealing to his listeners' understanding. I looked away to the lights of passing automobiles. I tried not to hear anymore. (p. 15)

In contrast to the alienation he felt when he heard his father speaking English, he felt comfort when members of his family spoke to him in Spanish:

> A family member would say something to me and I would feel specially recognized. My parents would say something to me and I would feel embraced by the sounds of their words. Those words said: I am speaking with ease in Spanish. I am addressing you in words I never use with los gringos. I recognize you as someone special, close, like no one outside. You belong with us. In the family. (p. 15, italics omitted)

Another way language affects our identity is through the labels we use to define ourselves. To illustrate, in the example above, I used the label "North American" to refer to my cultural identity. The fact that I did not use the label "American" tells you something about the way I see myself as a cultural being.

The labels individuals use regarding their ethnic group membership can tell us a lot about their orientations.[9] A person who labels himself a Chicano (female would be Chicana), for example, defines himself differently than a person who uses the label Mexican-American. To communicate effectively with either individual, it would be important to know why she or he chooses the label he or she does.

To further illustrate the importance of labels, we can look at research Michael Hecht and Sidney Ribeau (in press) conducted with blacks in the United States. They found that individuals use the label Black because it is "acceptable" and "based on consensus" (in the larger culture). Blacks report being willing to talk, being verbally aggressive, and using slang. Blacks also describe themselves as patriotic, accepting of the status quo, and attempting to assimilate into the larger culture. Individuals who use the label Black-Americans, in contrast, gain their identity from being both black and American. Like Blacks, Black-Americans attempt to assimilate into the larger culture. Black-Americans' communication style, however, is characterized by the use of dialect and code-switching. Afro-Americans also derive their identity from being black and American, but they do not want to assimilate into the larger culture, only succeed in it. Afro-Americans report that their communication style is distinguished by the use of ethnic forms of nonverbal communication and the use of black dialect.

ASSESSING YOUR CULTURAL AND ETHNIC IDENTITIES

In order to assist you in assessing the degree to which you generally identify with your cultural and ethnic group, two short questionnaires are presented in Table 3.2. Take a few minutes to complete these questionnaires now.

The scores on the two questionnaires range from 5 to 25. The higher your score, the more you identify with your culture and ethnic group. Keep your scores in mind. In later chapters, I will discuss how the strength of your identification with these groups can influence your communication with members of other groups. The questionnaires only assess the strength of your identification with your culture and ethnic group. They do not assess what it means to be a member of this group.

Table 3.2 Assessing Your Cultural and Ethnic Identities

The purpose of these two short questionnaires is to help you think about the degree to which you identify with being a member of your culture and ethnic group. Respond to each statement by indicating the degree to which the statement is true regarding the way you typically think about yourself. When you think about yourself is the statement "Always False" (answer 1), "Mostly False" (answer 2), "Sometimes True and Sometimes False" (answer 3), "Mostly True" (answer 4), or "Always True" (answer 5)?

Cultural Identity

_____ 1. Being a member of my culture is important to me.

_____ 2. Thinking about myself as a member of my culture is central to how I define myself.

_____ 3. If I were born again, I would want to be born as a member of my culture.

_____ 4. I often think about being a member of my culture.

_____ 5. Being a member of my culture plays a large role in my life.

Ethnic Identity

_____ 1. If I were born again, I would want to be born as a member of my ethnic group.

_____ 2. Being a member of my ethnic group is important to me.

_____ 3. I often think about being a member of my ethnic group.

_____ 4. Being a member of my ethnic group plays a large role in my life.

_____ 5. Thinking about myself as a member of my ethnic group is central to how I define myself.

To find your "scores," add the numbers you wrote next to each of the statements. Compute separate scores for cultural and ethnic identity. Scores range from 5 to 25. The higher your score, the more you identify with the group.

SOURCE: Some of the items on these scales are adapted from Hofman's (1985) measures of "civic" and ethnic identities.

❏ Gender and Other Forms of Diversity

Our cultural and ethnic identities are only two of the social identities that influence the way we communicate. There are many other social identities that can be the source of misinterpretations and ineffective communication. These include, but are not limited to gender, disability, age, and gender orientation.

GENDER

One of the major social identities affecting our communication is our gender and the way we define our gender role. Most of the research and writing to date on gender-based social identity has focused on women's social identity (e.g., Skevington & Baker, 1989). Several important issues emerge from this research.

First, there are differences in how women define themselves depending on whether internal or external criteria for group memberships are used. There are no agreed upon external criteria for "womanhood" and when women compare their internal definitions with external criteria there is always an inconsistency. This inconsistency often leads to a feeling of marginality and an unsatisfactory social identity for women (Breakwell, 1979).

Second, women attach different meanings to the category woman. There are "traditional" women, for example, who identify strongly with their group, see their roles as preferable to men's roles, and accept the existing gender-roles (Condor, 1986). Susan Condor's (1986) research also clearly indicates that women subcategorize their group:

> I've got a lot of things in common with other women. Interests and such like. Of course, by "other women," I mean wives and mothers like me. Women with family commitments, not career girls.
>
> When I talk about "women," I am taking it for granted that you understand that I am talking about women with careers outside the home.

Women, therefore, may identify with each other based on gender group membership or in terms of personal characteristics (Gurin & Townsend, 1986).

Third, there are differences in the way men and women relate to the world that affect their social identities. Tajfel's (1978) original work on social identity focused on social identity as a cognitive process of differentiation and comparison. Several writers (e.g., Williams, 1984) point out that women's social identity is based on more communal processes than differentiation processes.[10] Further, "women are more inclined [than men] to value relationships with other people from groups other than their own" (Skevington, 1989, p. 56). This may suggest that men and women engage in intergroup behavior differently.[11]

Aaron Beck (1988) summarizes conversational differences between men and women that can lead to misinterpretations. He points out that women tend to see questions as a way of keeping a conversation going. Men, in contrast, see questions as requests for information. Second, women tend to make connections between what their partner said and what they have to say. Men, on the other hand, do not use conversational "bridges" as much and may appear to ignore what their partners just said in a conversation. Third, men tend to view "aggressiveness" as a way of communicating, while women tend to interpret aggressiveness as an "attack." Women may discuss "problems" and only be looking for reassurances. Men, on the other hand, interpret the discussion of a problem as a request for a solution.[12]

While the differences between men and women outlined above may be overgeneralizations, they illustrate that women and men approach conversations with different expectations. When these expectations are violated, misinterpretations of the partner's messages often occur.[13]

OTHER FORMS OF DIVERSITY

Another factor that can affect our communication is whether or not the other person is "disabled." Research suggests that we categorize others based on their physical appearance and evaluate "novel" appearance negatively (McArthur, 1982). When nondisabled people communicate with people who are visibly disabled in some way, they tend to experience uncertainty and anxiety, and avoid interaction when possible.[14] Similar observations can be made about interactions with other people who we view as "stigmatized" (e.g., AIDS victims, mentally ill, etc.).

Members of other groups do not have to be visually disabled for us to experience uncertainty and anxiety and want to avoid communicating with them; for example, "young" people often avoid communicating with "old" people and heterosexuals often avoid homosexuals. One of the major group memberships causing conflict in the world today is religion. The protestants and catholics continue to fight in Northern Ireland and there has been an upsurge of anti-Semitism in the world recently.[15]

No matter what the criteria for strangers' group memberships, we do not have scripts to follow when communicating with them. The only basis we have for communicating with strangers is their group memberships and our stereotypes about their groups. Our stereotypes tend to provide us with "negative" expectations and we, therefore, try to avoid (either consciously or unconsciously) communicating with people who are different.

In the next chapter, I discuss the role of expectations in communication. Specifically, I examine positive versus negative expectations and how they influence our predictions of others' behavior and our interpretations of the messages we receive from them. I also look at specific factors on which our expectations are based including others' group memberships, our stereotypes, intergroup attitudes (e.g., prejudice, ethnocentrism, and racism), and our perceptions of similarity.

4

Our Expectations of Strangers

In the previous chapters, I indicated that we have expectations about how others are going to communicate. Sometimes we are highly aware of our expectations and sometimes we are not. In this chapter, I discuss expectations in detail. I begin by examining the nature of expectations. I then look at specific sources of our expectations for others' behavior focusing on those sources that contribute to misinterpretations and misunderstandings when we communicate with strangers.

❑ The Nature of Expectations

Expectations involve our anticipations and predictions about how others will communicate with us. Our expectations are derived from social norms, communication rules, and others' personal characteristics of which we are aware. Expectations also emerge from our intergroup attitudes and the stereotypes we hold. Intergroup attitudes and stereotypes are given more weight when we are communicating with people who are different and/or unknown than when we communicate with people who are similar and/or known.

EXPECTATIONS ARE CULTURALLY BASED

There is a "should" component to most of our expectations. "People who interact develop expectations about each others' behavior, not only in the sense that they are able to predict the regularities, but also in the sense that they develop preferences about how others *should* behave under certain circumstances" (Jackson, 1964, p. 225). Our culture and ethnicity provide guidelines for appropriate behavior and the expectations we use in judging competent communication. To illustrate, Judee Burgoon and Jerold Hale (1988) point out that in the white middle-class subculture[1]

> one expects normal speakers to be reasonably fluent and coherent in their discourse, to refrain from erratic movements or emotional outbursts, and to adhere to politeness norms. Generally, normative behaviors are positively valued. If one keeps a polite distance and shows an appropriate level of interest in one's conversational partner, for instance, such behavior should be favorably received. (p. 61)

The problem is that norms for what is a "polite" distance and what constitutes an "emotional" outburst vary across cultures and subcultures within a culture.

An example may help clarify the "problems" that occur when people from different cultures communicate. In the white middle-class subculture of the United States, we expect that friends will stand an acceptable distance away from us when talking (e.g., an arm's length away). Arabs, in contrast, expect friends to stand close enough so that they can smell each others' breath. To deny the smell of your breath to a friend is considered an insult in most Arab cultures. If a white from the United States and an Arab are following their own cultural norms and are not aware that the other person's norm is different, they will inevitably misinterpret each others' behavior.

When we are communicating with other members of our culture and/or ethnic group we usually are not aware of the norms and communication rules guiding our behavior. Following the norm or rule does not require effort or conscious thought (i.e., we follow the norms and rules we learned as children). Violating a norm or rule, in contrast, requires effort and thought. We also become aware of the norms and rules guiding our behavior when they are violated and we do not have a "ready made" interpretation for the violation.

Consider the example of shaking hands. Take a minute and think of the rules for shaking hands in the white middle-class subculture of the United States. In all likelihood, you thought of some, but not all of the rules. If we shake hands and my grip is not "firm," you do not stop and think "his grip is not firm." No, you will probably interpret my behavior, not describe it. Because you have "ready made" interpretations for a "limp" grip during a handshake, you may not realize I violated a norm. If we are shaking hands and I do not stop shaking your hands after several "pumps," however, you will probably think to yourself, "doesn't he know when to stop?" In this case you will probably recognize that I am violating the norm because there is no "ready made" interpretation for the way I violated the norm.

EVALUATING VIOLATIONS OF OUR EXPECTATIONS

If one person violates another's expectations to a sufficient degree that the violation is recognized, the person recognizing the violation becomes aroused and has to assess the situation (Burgoon & Hale, 1988). In other words, the violation of expectations leads to some degree of mindfulness.

Burgoon and Hale argue that the degree to which the other person provides us with rewards affects how we evaluate the violation and the person committing the act. As used here, rewards do not refer to money (although it might be a consideration if the other person is our boss or a client). Rather, rewards include the benefits we obtain from our interactions with the other person. If the other person provides us with rewards, we choose the most positive of the possible interpretations of violations that have multiple possible interpretations; "for example, increased proximity during conversation may be taken as a sign of affiliation if committed by a high reward person but as a sign of aggressiveness if committed by a low reward person" (Burgoon & Hale, 1988, p. 63).

> *We often believe our expectations have been fulfilled when we communicate with strangers, regardless of how the stranger behaves.*

According to Burgoon and Hale, "positively" evaluated violations of our expectations should have "positive" consequences for our communication with violators (e.g., not lead to misinterpretations, increase intimacy). "Negatively" evaluated violations, in contrast, generally lead to "negative" outcomes (e.g., misinterpretations, decreases in intimacy). There are, however, exceptions for negative violations. Burgoon and Hale point out that if the other person provides rewards and commits an extreme violation of our expectations, positive outcomes (e.g., higher credibility and/or interpersonal attraction) are possible.

Walter Stephan (1985) reviews research on the confirmation and disconfirmation of expectations when we communicate with strangers. He concludes that we often believe our expectations have been fulfilled when we communicate with strangers, regardless of how the stranger behaves. Stephan suggests that we tend not to change our behavior when others disconfirm our expectations. He goes on to point out that the

affective consequences of confirmation or disconfirmation depend to a great degree on whether the expectancy is positive or negative. Confirmation of positive expectancies and disconfirmation of negative expectancies would be expected to elicit favorable affective responses to the behavior, such as pride and happiness. Disconfirmation of positive expectancies and confirmation of negative expectancies may lead to negative affect, such as sadness or low self-esteem or resentment and hostility directed toward the self or the holder of the expectancy. (p. 637)

As Burgoon and Hale point out, however, whether the other person can provide rewards influences how we interpret the confirmation or disconfirmation of our expectations.

Before proceeding, it is important to point out that strangers with whom we communicate usually are not viewed as potential sources of rewards. Rather, we tend to see the costs as outweighing the rewards when we communicate with strangers. There are exceptions, however. Mark Knapp points out that interacting with people who are different "is enjoyable when the interaction is brief, when the differences are few and on peripheral beliefs, and when the chance of rejection is small, that is, when the costs of pursuing dissimilar relations are negligible relative to the rewards" (cited in Crockett & Friedman, 1980, p. 91).

NEGATIVE INTERGROUP EXPECTATIONS

Communication with strangers usually is based on negative expectations. Research indicates, for example, that actual or anticipated interaction with a member of a different ethnic group leads to anxiety.[2] As indicated in Chapter 1, Walter Stephan and Cookie Stephan (1985) argue we fear four types of negative consequences when interacting with strangers.

First, we fear negative consequences for our self-concepts. In interacting with strangers, we worry "about feeling incompetent, confused, and not in control. . . . anticipate discomfort, frustration, and irritation due to the awkwardness of intergroup interactions" (Stephan & Stephan, 1985, p. 159). We also may fear the loss of self-esteem, that our social identities will be threatened, and that we will feel guilty if we behave in ways that offend strangers.

Second, we may fear negative behavioral consequences will result from our communication with strangers. We may feel that strangers will exploit us, take advantage of us, or try to dominate us. We also may worry about performing poorly in the presence of strangers or worry that physical harm or verbal conflict will occur.

Third, we fear negative evaluations of strangers. We fear rejection, ridicule, disapproval, and being stereotyped negatively. These negative evaluations, in turn, can be seen as threats to our social identities. Recent research suggests that we perceive interpersonal communication as more agreeable and less abrasive than intergroup communication (Hoyle, Pinkley, & Insko, 1989).

Finally, we may fear negative evaluations by members of our ingroups. If we interact with strangers, members of our ingroups may disapprove. We may fear that "ingroup members will reject" us, "apply other sanctions," or identify us "with the outgroup" (Stephan & Stephan, 1985, p. 160).

Stephan and Stephan (1985) point out that "intergroup anxiety often has a basis in reality. People sometimes do make embarrassing mistakes, are taken advantage of, and are rejected by ingroup and outgroup members" (p. 160) when communicating with strangers. One of the emotional reactions we have to our expectations of strangers being disconfirmed is that we become frustrated. "Frustration involves feelings of intense discomfort stemming from the blockage of paths toward goals. . . . Frustration, in turn, often leads to aggressive behavior or people try to vent their negative feelings" (Brislin, Cushner, Cherrie, & Yong, 1986, p. 250).

The anxiety we experience when communicating with strangers is largely unconscious. To be managed, it must be brought to a conscious level (i.e., we must become mindful). To understand strangers, we must cognitively manage our anxiety.

Several factors appear to be associated with the amount of intergroup anxiety we experience. Thinking about the behavior in which we need to engage when communicating with strangers, for example, can reduce our anxiety about interacting with them (Janis & Mann, 1977). Further, if we focus on finding out as much as we can and forming accurate impressions of strangers, the biases we have based on our anxiety and negative expectations will be reduced (Leary, Kowalski, & Bergen, 1988; Neuberg, 1989). Stephan and Stephan (1989) also found that the less the intergroup contact we have experienced, the less ethnocentric we are, and the more positive our stereotypes are, the less the intergroup anxiety we experience.

❑ Intergroup Attitudes

"An attitude is a learned predisposition to respond in an evaluative (from extremely favorable to extremely unfavorable) manner toward some attitude object" (Davidson & Thompson, 1980, p. 27). I focus on two specific attitudes that affect or communication with strangers: ethnocentrism and prejudice.

ETHNOCENTRISM

William Graham Sumner (1940) defined ethnocentrism as "the view of things in which one's own group is the center of everything, and all others are scaled and rated with reference to it" (p. 13). According to Robert LeVine and Donald Campbell (1972), there are two facets to ethnocentrism. One involves our orientation toward our ingroup. If we are highly ethnocentric, we see our ingroup as virtuous and superior, and we see our ingroup values as universal (i.e., applying to everyone). The second facet of ethnocentrism involves our orientation toward outgroups. If we are highly ethnocentric, we see outgroups as contemptible and inferior, we reject outgroups' values, we blame outgroups for ingroup troubles, and we try to maintain social distance from outgroups.

We can think about ethnocentrism as the tendency to interpret and evaluate others' behavior using our own standards.

This tendency is natural and unavoidable. Everyone is ethnocentric to some degree. While it is possible to have a low degree of ethnocentrism, it is impossible to be nonethnocentric.

Ethnocentrism leads us to view our ways of doing things as the natural and "right" ways of doing things. The major consequence of this in an intergroup context is that we tend to view our ingroup way of doing things as "superior" to the outgroup's way of doing things. In other words, ethnocentrism is a bias toward the ingroup that causes us to evaluate different patterns of behavior negatively, rather than try to understand them.

One of the consequences of ethnocentrism is the way we talk to people who are different. Janet Lukens (1978) isolated three types of ethnocentric speech:

> (1) to demonstrate lack of concern for persons of other cultures and reflect an insensitivity to cultural differences (the distance of indifference), (2) to avoid or limit the amount of interaction with outgroups (the distance of avoidance), and (3) to demonstrate feelings of hostility towards outgroups and to deride or belittle them (the distance of disparagement). (p. 41)

Lukens contends that these three distances are associated with low, moderate, and high levels of ethnocentrism, respectively.

An example of speech at the distance of indifference is "foreigner talk." This usually takes the form of loud, slow, simplified speech patterns, with exaggerated pronunciation. Lukens argues that the use of ingroup dialect or jargon is a major technique used to establish the distance of avoidance. The distance of disparagement is characterized by the use of pejorative expressions and ethnophaulisms (e.g., name-calling and/or slurs; for example, "Jew them down," "honkey," etc.).

In *Communicating with Strangers* (Gudykunst & Kim, 1984), Young Yun Kim and I suggested that this view of "ethnocentric speech" is incomplete. If we think of ethnocentrism as a continuum ranging from low to high, low ethnocentrism should be manifested in a tendency to treat members of other groups as equal. Lukens' distance of indifference, therefore, would fall in the center of the continuum (moderate ethnocentrism; the other distances reflect moderately high and high ethnocentrism). Moving from the center toward the low end, moderately low ethnocentrism is reflected in a "distance of sensitivity." Speech at this distance reflects a desire to decrease the communicative distance between us and people who are different.

We are all prejudiced to some degree.

The "distance of equality" would be found at the low end of the continuum. At this distance, our speech is designed to demonstrate that we are trying to interpret others' behavior in terms of their culture. We are using descriptive, not evaluative statements.

When we are communicating on automatic pilot, most of us use one of Lukens' three communicative distances and are not highly aware of it. Communicating at one of these three distances inevitably leads to misinterpreting messages received from people who are different. If our goal is effective communication, we must become mindful of our communication and move toward the distance of equality in our style of communication.

ASSESSING YOUR ETHNOCENTRISM

Table 4.1 contains a brief questionnaire designed to help you assess your level of ethnocentrism. Take a moment to complete the questionnaire. In responding to the statements, please keep in mind it will not help you to understand your communication behavior if you answer the questions as you think you should. For the questionnaire to be useful, the questions must be answered honestly.

Scores on the questionnaire range from 5 to 25. The higher your score, the more ethnocentric you are. I will not provide "average" scores because they would not be useful in helping you improve your communication. The thing to keep in mind

Table 4.1 Assessing Your Ethnocentrism

The purpose of this questionnaire is to assess your ethnocentrism. Respond to each statement by indicating the degree to which the statement is true regarding the way you typically think about yourself. When you think about yourself, is the statement "Always False" (answer 1), "Mostly False" (answer 2), "Sometimes True and Sometimes False" (answer 3), "Mostly True" (answer 4), or "Always True" (answer 5)? Answer honestly, not how you think you should be.

_____ 1. I apply my values when judging people who are different.

_____ 2. I see people who are similar to me as virtuous.

_____ 3. I do not cooperate with people who are different.

_____ 4. I prefer to associate with people who are like me.

_____ 5. I do not trust people who are different.

To find your score, add the numbers you wrote next to each of the statements. Scores range from 5 to 25. The higher the score, the more ethnocentric you are.

SOURCE: The items on this questionnaire are drawn from Brewer's (1981) description of ethnocentrism.

is that the more ethnocentric you are, the more likely you are to misinterpret messages from strangers.

PREJUDICE

Prejudice involves making a prejudgment based on membership in a category. While prejudice can be positive or negative, there is a tendency for most of us to think of it as negative. Consistent with this view, Gorden Allport (1954) defined negative ethnic prejudice as "an antipathy based on a faulty and unflexible generalization. It may be felt or expressed. It may be irected toward a group as a whole, or toward an individual because he [or she] is a member of that group" (p. 10).

We tend to think of prejudice in terms of a dichotomy; either I am prejudiced or I am not. It is more useful, however, to think of the strength of our prejudice as varying along a continuum from low to high. This suggests that we all are prejudiced to some degree. We also are all racist, sexist, agist, and so forth to some degree. As with ethnocentrism, this is natural and unavoidable. It is the result of our being socialized as members of our ingroups. Even people with low levels of prejudice prefer to interact with people who are similar to themselves because such interactions are more comfortable and less stressful than interactions with strangers.

We also can think of prejudice as varying along a second continuum ranging from very positive to very negative. We tend to be positively prejudiced toward our ingroup and negatively prejudiced toward outgroups. It is possible, however, to be positively prejudiced toward outgroups and negatively prejudiced toward an ingroup. The valence (positive or negative) of our prejudice must be taken into consideration in trying to understand our reactions to violations of our expectations.

In today's society, it generally is not acceptable to make overt prejudiced comments in public.[3] It may be acceptable within some ingroups, but in public talk people try to present themselves as "nonprejudiced." If we are going to make a negative comment about people who are different, we preface our comment with a claim of not being prejudiced. To illustrate, one interviewee in Teun van Dijk's (1984) study responded in this way:

[INTERVIEWER]:   Did you ever have any unpleasant experiences [with foreigners]?
[INTERVIEWEE]:   I have nothing against foreigners. But their attitude, their aggression is scaring. We are no longer free here. You have to be careful. (p. 65)

van Dijk found that prejudiced talk clusters in four categories: (1) "they are different (culture, mentality)"; (2) "they do not adapt themselves"; (3) "they are involved in negative acts (nuisance, crime)"; and (4) "they threaten our (social, economic) interests" (p. 70). While van Dijk did his study in the Netherlands, these same types of prejudiced talk consistently are overheard in the United States.[4]

The way we talk about people who are different is, in large part, a function of how we want to be seen by our ingroup. van Dijk (1984) points out that people "adapt" their discourse to the rules and constraints of interaction and communication social settings. Especially when delicate topics, such as "foreigners," are concerned, social members will strategically try to realize both the aims of positive self-presentation and those of effective persuasion. Both aims, however, derive from the position of social members within their group. Positive self-presentation is not just a defense mechanism of individuals as persons, but also as respected, accepted, and integrated social members of ingroups. And the same holds for the persuasive nature of prejudiced talk; people do not merely lodge personal complaints or uneasiness about people of other groups, but intend to have their experiences, their evaluations, their opinions, their attitudes, and their actions shared by other members of the ingroup. (p. 154)

Everyone engages in prejudiced talk to some degree. It is inevitable. We can, however, reduce the degree to which we engage in prejudiced talk if we are mindful of our communication.

ASSESSING YOUR PREJUDICE

Table 4.2 contains a questionnaire designed to assess your level of prejudice. Take a couple of minutes to complete it now. Answer the questions honestly.

The higher your score on the questionnaire, the greater your level of prejudice. Everyone will be prejudiced to some degree. This is unavoidable. The important thing to keep in mind is that we can manage how our prejudices influence our communication by being mindful when we communicate with strangers.

❏ Stereotypes

Stereotypes result from our social categorizations. They are the "pictures" we have for the various social categories we use. Miles Hewstone and Rupert Brown (1986) isolate three essential aspects of stereotypes:

Table 4.2 Assessing Your Prejudice

The purpose of this questionnaire is to assess your prejudice. Respond to each statement by indicating the degree to which the statement is true regarding the way you typically think about other groups. When you think about other groups, is the statement "Always False" (answer 1), "Mostly False" (answer 2), "Sometimes True and Sometimes False" (answer 3), "Mostly True" (answer 4), or "Always True" (answer 5)? Answer honestly, not how you think you should be.

_____ 1. I do not think that discrimination against other groups is a problem today.

_____ 2. I think that members of other groups are too demanding in their push for equal rights.

_____ 3. I think that members of other groups have received more attention in the media than they deserve.

_____ 4. I do not understand why members of other groups are angry at my group.

_____ 5. I think that members of other groups should not push themselves-where they are not wanted.

To find your score, add the numbers you wrote next to each statement. Scores range from 5 to 25. The higher your score, the greater your prejudice.

SOURCE: The items on this questionnaire are adapted from McConahay's (1986) modern racism scale.

1 Often individuals are categorized, usually on the basis of easily identifiable characteristics such as sex or ethnicity.

2 A set of attributes is ascribed to all (or most) members of that category. Individuals belonging to the stereotyped group are assumed to be similar to each other, and different from other groups, on this set of attributes.

3 The set of attributes is ascribed to any individual member of that category. (p. 29)

Like ethnocentrism and prejudice, stereotyping is a natural result of the communication process. We cannot not stereotype. Henri Tajfel (1981) draws a distinction between stereotypes and social stereotypes:

"Stereotypes" are certain generalizations reached by individuals. They derive in large measure from, or are an instance of, the general cognitive process of categorizing. The main function of the process is to simplify or systematize, for purposes of cognitive and behavioral adaptation, the abundance and complexity of the information received from its environment by the human organism. . . . But such stereotypes can become *social* only when they are shared by large numbers of people within social groups. (pp. 146-147)

Some of our stereotypes are unique and based on our individual experiences, but some are shared with other members of our ingroups. The stereotypes we share with others are our social stereotypes. We may know what the social stereotype of a group is, but still hold a different view of the group (Devine, 1989).

Our stereotypes are multidimensional images.[5] They vary in terms of their complexity (e.g., the number of traits included), specificity (e.g., how specific the traits are), favorability (e.g., the positive or negative valence of the traits), the degree of consensus there is on the traits, and whether or not they are valid (Vassiliou et al., 1972).

STEREOTYPING AND COMMUNICATION

Stereotypes provide the content of our social categories. We have social categories in which we place people and it is our stereotype that tells us what people in that category are like.[6] We can draw at least four generalizations about the stereotyping process (Hewstone & Giles, 1986).[7] First, stereotyping is the result of our tendency to overestimate the degree of association between group membership and psychological attributes. While there may be some association between group membership and psychological characteristics of members, it is much smaller than we assume when we communicate on automatic pilot.

Second, stereotypes influence the way we process information. Research indicates that we remember more favorable information about our ingroups and more unfavorable information about outgroups. This, in turn, affects the way we interpret incoming messages from members of ingroups and outgroups.

Third, stereotypes create expectations regarding how members of other groups will behave. Stereotypes are activated automatically when we have contact with strangers (Devine, 1989). Unconsciously, we assume that our expectations are correct and behave as though they are. We, therefore, try to confirm our expectations when we communicate with members of other groups. We can, however, control the effects of automatic processing. This occurs especially in conditions where we want to present a "nonprejudiced" identity (Devine, 1989).

Fourth, our stereotypes constrain others' patterns of communication and engender stereotype-confirming communication. Stated differently, stereotypes create self-fulfilling prophecies. We tend to see behavior that confirms our expectations, even when it is absent. We ignore disconfirming evidence when communicating on automatic pilot. If we assume someone else is not competent and communicate with them based on this assumption, they will appear incompetent (even if they are actually competent).

ASSESSING YOUR STEREOTYPES

To get an idea of what your stereotypes are, take a few minutes and complete the questionnaire in Table 4.3. To complete this questionnaire you need to think of a specific group to which you belong (your culture or ethnic group) and another group (another culture or ethnic group).

The specific adjectives you check constitute the content of your stereotype. The content of your stereotypes can vary in complexity (i.e., the number of traits), but I limited your selection to five traits on the questionnaire. The content also can vary in terms of the degree of consensus (i.e., do other members of your group assign the same traits to your group) and "validity" (i.e., do members of the other group assign the same traits to themselves as you assign to them).

Table 4.3 Assessing Your Stereotypes

The purpose of this questionnaire is to help you understand what your stereotypes of your own and other groups are. Several adjectives are listed below. Because stereotypes are specific to particular groups, you will have to think of specific groups. Think of one group of which you are a member (e.g., your cultural or ethnic group) and an outgroup (e.g., another culture or ethnic group). Put a check mark in the column "My Group" next to the five adjectives that apply to your group. Put a check mark in the column marked "Other Group" next to the five adjectives that apply to the outgroup you have selected. After you put your check marks, go back through the list and rate each adjective you checked in terms of how favorable of a quality the adjective is: 1 = very unfavorable, 2 = moderately unfavorable, 3 = neither favorable nor unfavorable, 4 = moderately favorable, and 5 = very favorable. Put these ratings in the column to the right of the adjectives.

My Group	Other Group		Favorableness
_____	_____	Intelligent	_____
_____	_____	Materialistic	_____
_____	_____	Ambitious	_____
_____	_____	Industrious	_____
_____	_____	Deceitful	_____
_____	_____	Conservative	_____
_____	_____	Practical	_____
_____	_____	Shrewd	_____
_____	_____	Arrogant	_____
_____	_____	Aggressive	_____
_____	_____	Sophisticated	_____
_____	_____	Conceited	_____
_____	_____	Neat	_____
_____	_____	Alert	_____
_____	_____	Impulsive	_____
_____	_____	Stubborn	_____
_____	_____	Conventional	_____
_____	_____	Progressive	_____
_____	_____	Sly	_____
_____	_____	Tradition-loving	_____
_____	_____	Pleasure-loving	_____

The adjectives you checked constitute the content of your stereotypes. To find out how favorable the stereotypes are add the numbers next to the adjectives checked. Compute separate favorableness scores for the stereotype of your group and the other group. Scores range from 5 to 25. The higher the score, the more favorable your stereotype.

SOURCE: The list of adjectives is adapted from Katz and Braly (1933).

TYPICAL AND ATYPICAL GROUP MEMBERS

Stereotypes are "pictures" of a category or group. Individual members of a group may or may not fit a stereotype, however. Stella Ting-Toomey (1989) isolated four possible options between how individuals identify with a group and the way they behave: (1) individuals may see themselves as a typical group member and behave typically, (2) individuals may see themselves as a typical group member and behave atypically, (3) individuals may see themselves as atypical group members and behave atypically, and (4) individuals may see themselves as atypical group members and behave typically. Each of these ways that people present themselves has different consequences for accurately interpreting the behavior of people who are different. The accuracy of my expectations also depends on whether the traits that I include in my stereotype of your group are similar to the ones in your stereotype of your group (i.e., are my stereotypes valid). If the traits I apply to your group agree with the traits members of your group apply to themselves, my stereotype should lead to accurate interpretations of the behavior of members of the group who are "typical." "Valid" stereotypes, however, will lead to misinterpretations of the behavior of "atypical" members of the group.

Stereotypes, in and of themselves, do not lead to miscommunication and/or communication breakdown. If, however, inaccurate stereotypes are held rigidly, they lead to inaccurate predictors of others' behavior and misunderstandings. In addition to inaccurate stereotypes, simple stereotypes of other groups can lead to misunderstandings. In order to increase our effectiveness in communicating with strangers, we need to increase the complexity of our stereotypes and question our unconscious assumption that most members of a group fit a single stereotype (Stephan & Rosenfield, 1982).

Patricia Devine (1989) argues that conscious control of our reactions when our stereotypes are activated is necessary to control our prejudice:

> Nonprejudiced responses are . . . a function of intentional con-
> trolled processes and require a conscious decision to behave in
> a nonprejudiced fashion. In addition, new responses must be
> learned and well practiced before they can serve as competitive
> responses to the automatically activated stereotype-congruent
> response. (p. 15)

This position is consistent with Langer's notion that mindfulness is necessary to reduce prejudice.

STEREOTYPES AND "COMMUNICATION BREAKDOWNS"

Miles Hewstone and Howard Giles (1986) developed a
stereotype-based model of intergroup communication breakdown. They define communication breakdown as a feeling of
dissatisfaction that detracts from the full potential of an encounter. For the breakdown to be intergroup in nature, the
individuals must attribute their dissatisfaction as being due to
membership in contrasting social groups.

Hewstone and Giles (1986) begin by focusing on the context
in which we communicate with strangers. Context involves the
historical and changing relationship between social groups. It
includes the past efforts that members of different groups have
made toward mutual social and linguistic accommodation. Accommodation refers to our tendency to adapt our behavior to
others' behavior. We can move toward others or move away
from them. Using our own language when around people who
do not speak it is one way we may exert a positive social
identity (Giles, Bourhis, & Taylor, 1977). We tend to react favor-
ably to outgroup members who linguistically move toward us
(e.g., speak our language or dialect).[8] Our reaction, however,
depends upon the intent we attribute to the speaker. Hewstone
and Giles suggest that as mutual convergence increases, there
is less of a likelihood of communication breakdowns occurring.

Another contextual factor that may influence communication breakdowns we have with strangers is the changes in the
sociostructural positions of the different groups in society.
As we perceive that the members of other groups are making

evaluative comparisons with our group, there is an increased potential for communication breakdowns to occur.

Our perceptions of the situation and of the characteristics of strangers with whom we are communicating (e.g., are there more strangers than people we know present? are the strangers typical of their group?) affects how important social identifications are in the encounter. Our stereotypes of outgroup members lead us to depersonalize them (i.e., think of them as members of a group and not as individuals). When this occurs, we place less emphasis on the individual characteristics of outgroup members because the stereotypes associated with the groups are guiding our behavior. Hewstone and Giles draw upon Gudykunst and Kim's (1984) extension of Lukens' (1978) work on communicative distances. Hewstone and Giles contend that when intergroup communication occurs at the "distance of sensitivity," speakers may attempt to accommodate each other. They go on to argue that as we use our stereotypes in intergroup conflicts, our communication patterns are affected negatively by the stereotypes we hold. We use our stereotypes of outgroups to explain communication difficulties and, therefore, confirm our negative feelings associated with the outgroup. Hewstone and Giles speculate that participants in intergroup breakdowns are likely to seek advice and consolation of members of the ingroup and, therefore, they will ultimately attribute the cause of the breakdown to the outgroup members.

In applying Hewstone and Giles' model, the speech norms of the context must be taken into consideration. The content of speech norms varies from situation to situation, but deviation from or adherence to the norms conveys important information about ourselves and others (McKirnan & Hamayan, 1984). We can, for example, "negotiate" specific identities by choosing to violate speech norms in a particular situation (Scotton, 1980). A Japanese-American who is fluent in Japanese, for example, can define his or her identity as Japanese-American, not Japanese, by speaking English when she or he is introduced to Japanese.

❑ Changing Our Intergroup Expectations

Marilyn Brewer and Norman Miller (1988) argue that when we communicate with strangers there are three ways that our experiences with individual strangers can generalize to change our attitudes toward their groups:

> 1. *Change in attitudes toward the group as a whole.* This is the most direct form of generalization, where positive experiences with individual members of a broad social category lead to alterations in the affect and stereotypes associated with the group as a whole.
> 2. *Increased complexity of intergroup perceptions.* This form of generalization involves a change in the perceived heterogeneity of category structure. Instead of perceiving the out-group category as a relatively homogeneous social group, the individual comes to recognize variability among category members. Attitudes toward the category as a whole may not be altered, but affect and stereotypes are differentiated among various "sub-types" of the general category.
> 3. *Decategorization.* In this form of generalization, the meaningfulness of the category itself is undermined. Based on the frequency or intensity of exposure to individual members of a social group, the utility of category membership as a basis for identifying or classifying new individuals is reduced. (p. 316)

Each of these forms of generalization deserve brief discussion.

CHANGE IN ATTITUDES TOWARD THE GROUP AS A WHOLE

Many people assume that if we have contact with members of other groups, our attitudes toward those groups will become more positive. This, however, is not necessarily the case. Research on intergroup contact suggests that contact can promote better relations between groups or increase hostility between groups. The question that needs to be answered is when does contact lead to better relations between groups?

In his review of research on intergroup contact, Walter Stephan (1985) isolated 13 characteristics of the contact situation that are necessary for positive attitude change toward a social group to occur as a result of our individual contact with specific strangers:

1. Cooperation within groups should be maximized and competition between groups should be minimized.
2. Members of the in-group and the out-group should be of equal status both within and outside the contact situation.
3. Similarity of group members on nonstatus dimensions (beliefs, values, etc.) appears to be desirable.
4. Differences in competence should be avoided.
5. The outcomes should be positive.
6. Strong normative and institutional support for the contact should be provided.
7. The intergroup contact should have the potential to extend beyond the immediate situation.
8. Individuation of group members should be promoted.
9. Nonsuperficial contact (e.g., mutual disclosure of information) should be encouraged.
10. The contact should be voluntary.
11. Positive effects are likely to correlate with the duration of the contact.
12. The contact should occur in a variety of contexts with a variety of in-group and out-group members.
13. Equal numbers of in-group and out-group members should be used. (p. 643)

While this list is long, Stephan points out that it is incomplete. If we want to design a program to reduce prejudice or ethnocentrism, we, therefore, must make sure that the contact we arrange meets as many of these conditions as possible.

INCREASED COMPLEXITY OF INTERGROUP PERCEPTIONS

This form of generalization involves seeing the social category as heterogeneous, rather than homogeneous. Stated differently, we can increase the complexity of our intergroup perceptions by recognizing how members of a social category are different. Think of the social groups males and females. Are all males and all females the same? Obviously, the answer is no. We see differences among males and females and place them in subcategories. Females, for example, may categorize males into "male chauvinists" and "feminists."

Increasing the complexity of our intergroup perceptions is consistent with Langer's notion of mindfulness. As you may recall from Chapter 2, one aspect of becoming mindful of our communication is the creation of new categories. Creating new categories for Langer means differentiating among the individuals within the broad social categories we use. This mean increasing the number of "discriminations" we make—using specific rather than global labels (e.g., a person with a lame leg, rather than a "cripple"). When we are mindful of differences among the members of the various outgroups with whom we communicate, our expectations are based on the subcategories, not the broader social category.

DECATEGORIZATION

Decategorization occurs when we communicate with strangers based on their individual characteristics, rather than the categories in which we place them (i.e., communication is interpersonal, not intergroup). In order to accomplish this, we must differentiate individual strangers from their groups. Differentiation alone, however, is not sufficient for decategorization or personalization to occur.

When we personalize or decategorize our interactions with strangers, personal identity takes on more importance than social identity.

To illustrate this distinction, consider the statement

"Janet is a nurse." This description can be psychologically represented in one of two ways. It could mean that Janet is subordinate to (i.e., a specific instance of) the general category of nurses. Or it could mean that being a nurse is subordinate to (i.e., a particular characteristic of) the concept of Janet. The former interpretation is an example of category-based individuation, and the latter is an example of personalization. (Brewer & Miller, 1988, p. 318)

The difference lies in how we process the information. If we focus on the strangers' personal identities, we can decrease the degree to which their social identities affect our expectations.

Changing our attitudes toward outgroups, increasing the complexity of our intergroup perceptions, and decategorization can all change our expectations of strangers. To create positive expectations and improve our relations with members of other groups, we need to use all three processes simultaneously.

Changing our expectations of strangers is necessary for us to communicate effectively with them. To improve our communication effectiveness, we also need to understand how we make sense of strangers' behavior. This is the topic of the next chapter.

5

Attributing Meaning to Strangers' Behavior

In the previous chapter, I discussed how our expectations affect our communication behavior. In this chapter, I extend this analysis by looking at the way we make sense of our world—the attribution process. I examine the individual and social attribution processes and isolate factors that lead us to make errors in attributions. I also discuss the role of cultural and personality factors in the attribution process.

❑ The Attribution Process

INDIVIDUAL ATTRIBUTIONS

Fritz Heider (1958) originally raised the question of how we make sense of our own and others' behavior and how our

83

interpretations shape our responses to behavior. He believed that we act as "naive" or "intuitive" scientists when we are trying to make sense of the world. Briefly, Heider suggests that we are motivated by practical concerns such as our need to simplify and comprehend our environment, and to predict others' behavior. In order to meet these needs, we try to get beneath external appearances to isolate stable underlying processes which he called "dispositional properties." Heider believes that others' motives are the dispositions we use most frequently in giving meaning to our experiences. He also pointed out that it is not our experiences per se, but our interpretations of our experiences that constitute our "reality."

Harold Kelley (1967) extended Heider's work by trying to explain when we attribute behavior to internal causes and when we attribute it to external causes. He argues that when observing others' behavior we attempt to make attributions about the effect of the environment on their behavior by ruling out individual explanations for the behavior. We organize our observations into a cube with three dimensions: person X object X situation. In the person dimension, we compare the person engaging in the behavior with others; in the object dimension, we compare the different objects of the person's behavior; in the situation dimension, we vary the context in which the behavior occurs. We then use a "covariation" principle to assess the degree to which the behavior occurs in the presence and absence of the various causes.[1]

The analysis of covariation is based on several principles. The principle of consistency deals with the extent to which the behavior occurs across time and location, given the same stimulus. The distinctiveness principle involves the extent to which other objects bring about the same behavior. The consensus principle deals with the degree to which people other than the person involved engage in the same behavior.

To illustrate this process, consider the following example. Jane is one of three women involved in planning a conference. During the planning meetings, we notice that Jane is very concerned with details and in isolating anything that might go wrong. Our analysis would compare Jane's behavior in planning the conference across the different planning meetings in which we observe her (searching for consistency). For the purpose of the example, we will assume that Jane's behavior is consistent across time and location. Next, we examine Jane's behavior in other contexts (searching for distinctiveness). Our observations indicate that Jane pays attention to detail across different contexts. Finally, we compare Jane's behavior with that of the other two planners (searching for consensus). We observe that the other two are not as concerned with details of the conference and do not raise as many questions of what might go wrong as Jane. Given these observations, what do we conclude? The most likely conclusion is that Jane's personality is responsible for her behavior.

Attributing behavior to dispositional characteristics is enhanced when an outgroup member engages in negative behavior.

In the above example, it appears that the attributional process takes a long time. In actuality, we go through this analysis very quickly when we have complete information. While Kelley's attributional cube explains our attributions when we have complete information, it may not describe our everyday interactions when we do not have complete information. Kelley (1972) argues that in the presence of incomplete data, we infer meaning based on "theories" or preconceptions we have about how specific causes are associated with specific effects. Our causal schemata permit "economical and fast attributional analysis, by providing a framework within which bits and pieces of information can be fitted in order to draw reasonably good inferences" (p. 152).

Kelley (1967) also isolated several biases that affect our attributional processes. First, we have a tendency to overestimate the influence of personal, dispositional characteristics and underestimate the influence of situational factors when we make attributions. This is called the "fundamental attribution error" (Ross, 1977). Second, we tend to see our own behavior as normal and appropriate (the "egocentric" bias). We, therefore, explain others' behavior that is different as a function of their personal dispositions. Third, we tend to attribute our success to personal dispositions and our failures to situational factors (the "ego-protective" bias).

SOCIAL ATTRIBUTIONS

Heider's and Kelley's explanations of the individual attribution process do not take into account that we are members of social groups. It, therefore, is necessary to look at the influence of group memberships on the attribution process. When group membership is taken into consideration, the process is called social attributions. Social attributions are concerned with how members of one social group explain the behavior of their own members and members of other social groups.

Miles Hewstone and Joseph Jaspars (1984) isolate three propositions regarding the social nature of attributions:

(1) Attribution is social in origin (e.g., it may be created by, or strengthened through, social interaction, or it may be influenced by social information).

(2) Attribution is social in its reference or object (e.g., an attribution may be demanded for the individual characterized as a member of a social group, rather than in purely individual terms; or for a social outcome, rather than any behavior as such).

(3) Attribution is social in that it is common to the members of a society or group (e.g., the members of different groups may hold different attributions for the same event. (pp. 379-380; italics omitted)

Hewstone and Jaspars argue that we enhance our social identities when we make social attributions. They also point out that our social attributions usually are based on the social stereotypes we share with other members of our ingroups. Our social attributions, however, can also be based on ethnocentrism.

Miles Hewstone and Rupert Brown (1986) present a model of interpersonal and intergroup contact which includes attributions as a major component. They argue that when we perceive ourselves and others in individual terms (e.g., our personal identities generate our behavior) or we see an outgroup member as atypical, we tend to make person-based attributions. Person-based attributions, in turn, lead us to look for personal similarities and differences between us and the other person. When we perceive ourselves and others as members of groups (e.g., our social identities generate our behavior), we tend to make category-based attributions. Category-based attributions then lead us to look for differences between our ingroup and the relevant outgroup.

The nature of the attributions we make are important and can determine whether or not our relations with members of other groups will improve. When members of different groups are working together and fail on their task, members of the ingroup usually blame the outgroup for the failure. Attributions like this do not help to improve intergroup relations and can, in fact, have a negative influence. If ingroup members are somehow "prevented" from blaming the outgroup for the failure, cooperation that results in failure does not result in increased bias toward the outgroup (Worchel & Norwell, 1980).

THE ULTIMATE ATTRIBUTION ERROR

Thomas Pettigrew (1979) proposes that the "ultimate" attribution error is "a systematic patterning of intergroup misattributions shaped in part by prejudice" (p. 464). He points out that our tendency to attribute behavior to dispositional characteristics, especially group membership, is enhanced when a member of an outgroup is perceived to engage in negative behavior. When members of an outgroup engage in what is perceived to be positive behavior, in contrast, our tendency is to treat the person as an "exception to the rule" and we discount dispositional explanations for the behavior. We, therefore, attribute the behavior to situational factors.

When our expectations are confirmed by others' behavior, we rely on others' dispositions associated with our stereotype of their group and do not bother to consider other explanations for the behavior (Pyszczynski & Greenberg, 1981). When others do not confirm our expectations, we tend to attribute their behavior to external factors (Stephan & Rosenfield, 1982).

The ultimate attribution error is illustrated in a study of perceptions of "shoving" (Duncan, 1976). In this study, students were shown a videotape of one person (either a black or white) shoving another person (either a black or white). White respondents attributed the shoving to dispositional causes (i.e., race) when the person doing the shoving was black, but not when the person was white. The respondents also thought the shove was more "violent" when it was administered by a black than when administered by a white.

With respect to the ultimate attribution error, Pettigrew (1978) concluded that

> across-group perceptions are more likely than within-group perceptions to include the following:
>
> 1. For acts perceived as antisocial or undesirable, behavior will be attributed to personal, dispositional causes. Often these internal causes will be seen as innate characteristics, and role requirements will be overlooked. ("He shoved the white guy, because blacks are born violent like that.")
> 2. For acts perceived as prosocial or desirable, behavior will be attributed either: (a) to the situation—with role requirements receiving more attention ("Under the circumstances, what could the cheap Scot do, but pay the check?"); (b) to the motivational, as opposed to innate, dispositional qualities ("Jewish students make better grades, because they try so much harder"); or (c) to the exceptional, even exaggerated "special case" individual who is contrasted with his/her group—what Allport (1954) called "fence-mending" ("She is certainly bright and hardworking — not at all like other Chicanos").

(p. 39; italics omitted)

It is very likely that we will make the ultimate attribution error when communicating on automatic pilot. To reduce the possibility of making this error when making attributions about the behavior of strangers, we must be mindful of our interpretations of their behavior.

❑ Category Width

There is one individual difference ("personality") variable that appears to influence the nature of the attributions we make. "Category width refers to the range of instances included in a cognitive category" (Pettigrew, 1982, p. 200).[2] To illustrate, is a pane of glass in the wall that is one inch wide and 12 feet high a window? A "narrow categorizer" would probably say no, while a wide categorizer would probably say yes. Wide categorizers have more latitude than narrow categorizers in what they include in a category.

Richard Detweiler (1978) summarizes the differences in tendencies when he points out that category width

> is a term used to describe the amount of discrepancy tolerable among category members—how similar do things have to be to be called by the same name? A narrow categorizer might put only highly similar things in the same category, whereas a broad categorizer might put more discrepant things in the same category. (p. 263)

Pettigrew (1982) suggests that individual differences in category width are related to more general information processing strategies people use. Broad categorizers, for example, tend to perform better than narrow categorizers on tasks that require holistic, integrated information processing. Narrow categorizers, in comparison, tend to perform better than broad categorizers on tasks that require detailed, analytic information processing.

There are several other differences between narrow and broad categorizers that are worth noting. Milton Rokeach (1951), for example, found that broad categorizers include concepts like Buddhism, Capitalism, Christianity, Democracy, Judaism, and Socialism in the same category (e.g., beliefs or doctrines), while narrow categorizers do not. Rokeach also discovered that narrow categorizers are more ethnocentric than broad categorizers. Research further indicates that nar-

row categorizers "react more to change, seek less prior information, and are more confident of their performances" than broad
categorizers (Pettigrew, 1982, p. 207).

CATEGORY WIDTH AND INTERGROUP ATTRIBUTIONS

Detweiler (1975) studied how category width influences the
attributions whites in the United States make about people who
are culturally similar (another white from the United States) or
culturally dissimilar (a person from Haiti) who engage in either positive or negative behavior. His findings indicate that
narrow categorizers

> assume that the effects of behavior of a person from another
> culture tell all about the person, even though he [or she] in fact
> knows nothing about the actor's [or actress'] cultural back-
> ground. He [or she] seems to make strong judgments based on
> the positivity or negativity of the effects of the behavior as evalu-
> ated from his [or her] own cultural viewpoint. Contrarily, when
> making attributions to a person who is culturally similar, the
> narrow [categorizer] seems to view the similarity as overshadow-
> ing the behavior. Thus, positive effects are seen as intended, and
> negative effects are confidently seen as unintended. (p. 600)

These findings suggest that narrow categorizers may have trouble making accurate attributions about messages from both
people who are culturally similar and people who are culturally
dissimilar.

The wide categorizers in Detweiler's (1975) study had a very
different orientation. When making attributions about a culturally dissimilar person, a wide categorizer

> seems to assume that he [or she] in fact doesn't know enough to
> make "usual" attributions. Thus, behaviors with negative effect
> result in less confident and generally more neutral attributions
> when judgments are made about a person from a different culture.
> Conversely, the culturally similar person who causes a negative
> outcome is rated relatively more negatively with greater confi-
> dence by the wide [categorizer], since the behavior from one's own
> cultural background is meaningful. (p. 600)

Given these findings, wide categorizers are more likely than narrow categorizers to search for the "appropriate" interpretation of a culturally dissimilar person's behavior.

The results of Detweiler's study may sound like they are due to ethnocentrism or tolerance of ambiguity and not category width, but this is not the case. He measured ethnocentrism and tolerance for ambiguity and looked at their effects on attributions. Detweiler's findings suggest that it is category width that actually effects the attributions we make.

What are the implications of this research on category width for our communication with people who are different? Narrow categorizers need to recognize that they will assume that they have sufficient information to make an attribution about people who are different when they do not. This assumption, in turn, will lead them to make inaccurate attributions about the behavior of people from different cultures or ethnic groups. These tendencies, however, can be managed cognitively by becoming mindful when narrow categorizers communicate with people who are different.

ASSESSING YOUR CATEGORY WIDTH

Table 5.1 contains a questionnaire designed to help you assess your category width. Take a couple of minutes and complete it now.

Scores on the questionnaire range from 5 to 25. The higher your score, the broader your categories. The important thing to keep in mind is that lower scores suggest that you have a tendency to judge the behavior of people who are different using your own group's standards.

❑ Culture and Misattributions

The cultural and ethnic norms and rules for communication we learned as children often contribute to misunderstandings

Table 5.1 Assessing Your Category Width

The purpose of this questionnaire is to help you to assess your category width. Each statement contains two parts. The first part of the statement is accurate. You are to indicate how certain you are that the second part of the statement is true. If you are certain the statement is not correct, answer 1; if you think it very unlikely that the statement is correct, answer 2; if can not decide if the statement is correct or incorrect, answer 3; if you think it is very likely that the statement is correct, answer 4; if you are pretty certain that the statement is correct, answer 5.

_____ 1. It has been estimated that the average width of windows is 34 inches. The widest window known is 1,363 inches.

_____ 2. Boating experts estimate that the average speed of all sail boats is around 4.1 knots. The fastest sail boat can go 30.7 knots.

_____ 3. When all of the world's written languages are considered, linguists tell us that the average number of verbs per language is about 15,000. The language with the least number of verbs has less than 1,000.

_____ 4. It has been estimated that the average person spends 55 minutes a day eating. The longest time spent eating by one person is 245 minutes per day.

_____ 5. The average population of South American countries is over 10 million people per country. The country with the least population has less than 50,000 people.

To find your score, add the numbers in front of each statement. Scores range from 5 to 25. The higher your score, the wider your categories.

SOURCE: This instrument is adapted from Pettigrew (1958).

when we communicate with people who are different. It is not possible for me to discuss the full range of areas where misunderstandings might occur in a short book like this. I, therefore, have chosen to try to illustrate how misunderstandings occur by linking them to the dimensions of cultural variability discussed in Chapter 3. Understanding how individualism-collectivism and low- and high-context affect our communication can help us to make appropriate attributions when we communicate with people from different cultures.

INDIVIDUALISM-COLLECTIVISM

Members of collectivistic cultures are group-oriented and there is a strong identification with ingroups (i.e., groups with which people identify). In individualistic cultures, emphasis is placed on the self. The differences in the group- or self-orientation often leads to misinterpretations of the behavior of members of other cultures in the formation and development of interpersonal relationships between members of individual-istic and collectivistic cultures.

We can begin with a simple straight-forward example of the use of personal pronouns in individualistic and collectivistic cultures. A member of a collectivistic culture who identifies with the group, for example, may offer personal opinions by using the pronoun "we" when stating a personal opinion. A member of an individualistic culture would perceive such a statement as being something that the group may do or believe, but not necessarily interpret the statement as the speaker's opinion. This misinterpretation will result in misunderstand-ing if the cultural differences in use of personal pronouns is ignored.

Another example of how differences in individualism-collectivism can lead to misunderstanding involves how face is negotiated. Face is defined as the public self-image (Ting-Toomey, 1988). Face can be based on our need for inclusion or our need for autonomy. Further, we can have a concern for our own face or a concern for another's face. Problems in commu-nication may occur when there is a difference in interpretation of the face-concern being used. In collectivistic cultures, the concern for face is predominately other-oriented. In individu-alistic cultures, the concern is self-oriented. Misunderstandings may occur when individualists fail to give face to collectivists when they interact.

The issue of giving face, especially to people with higher status, is important in collectivistic cultures. When people from individualistic cultures violate this expectation, it can have major consequences for their relationship. Richard Brislin and his associates (1986) present an example of this in the context of business negotiations between individuals in Japan and the United States:

> Phil Downing . . . was involved in the setting up of a branch of his company that was merging with an existing Japanese counterpart. He seemed to get along very well with the executive colleagues assigned to work with him, one of whom had recently been elected chairman of the board when his grandfather retired. Over several weeks discussion, they had generally laid out some working policies and agreed on strategies that would bring new directions needed for development. Several days later . . . the young chairman's grandfather happened to drop in. He began to comment on how the company had been formed and had been built up by the traditional practices, talking about some of the policies the young executives had recently discarded. Phil expected the new chairman to explain some of the new innovative and developmental policies they had both agreed upon. However, the young man said nothing; instead, he just nodded and agreed with his grandfather. Phil was bewildered and frustrated . . . and he started to protest. The atmosphere in the room became immediately tense . . . A week later the Japanese company withdrew from the negotiations. (pp. 155-156)

The young chairman of the Japanese company was giving his grandfather face by agreeing with him. This did not, however, negate any of the negotiations he had with Phil. Phil obviously did not understand this. By protesting and disagreeing with the grandfather, Phil not only failed to give face to the grandfather, he threatened the grandfather's face.

Face issues also can lead to misunderstanding in interethnic encounters in the United States. In the white, middle-class subculture, for example, refusing to comply with a directive given by a superior is attributed as a face threatening act. In the black subculture, however, "stylin" includes refusing to comply as part of a verbal "game" people play. This can be a problem when white teachers interact with black students and neither understands the others' communication style:

The white teachers, not realizing the play argument was a salient speech event in the children's speech community, took literally the child's refusal to comply, often with disastrous results for the child's reputation. Such children can be seen as recalcitrant and possibly emotionally disturbed [by white teachers]. (Erickson, 1981, pp. 6-7)

It also is possible for communicators from individualistic and collectivistic cultures to believe that they are using similar ideas, but mean different things. Tamar Katriel (1986) isolates major differences in what is perceived as *dugri* speech in Arabic (Arab cultures are collectivistic) and Hebrew (Israel is individualistic). *Dugri* speech can be defined loosely as a type of speech that is straight-forward and direct. The Hebrew use of *dugri* speech is centered around a report of the subjective experience, feelings and emotions. The Arabic use of *dugri* speech, on the other hand, is centered around objective observations of facts. This difference can easily lead to misunderstandings. Essential to the Hebrew uses of *dugri* speech is that the basic barrier to truth-speaking is a self-face concern. Concern for the self is seen as reflecting courage and integrity and *dugri* speech is used as a device to allow speakers to be truthful in expressing their feelings. In Arabic cultures, a high value is placed on smoothness of interpersonal relationships and *dugri* is used as a means to relay facts. Misunderstandings occur when the speakers of Hebrew-*dugri* and Arabic-*dugri* communicate and assume *dugri* means the same thing in both cultures.

LOW- AND HIGH-CONTEXT COMMUNICATION

Peter Erhenhaus (1983) argues that the types of attributions people make in low- and high-context cultures differ. Members of collectivistic, high-context cultures are sensitive to situational features and explanations, and tend to attribute others' behavior to the context, situation, or other factors external to the individual. Members of individualistic, low-context cultures, in contrast, are sensitive to dispositional characteristics

and tend to attribute others' behavior to characteristics internal
to the individual (e.g., personality).

Ehrenhaus' (1983) speculations are supported by recent research. Joan Miller (1984), for example, found that people in
India (high-context, collectivistic) make greater reference to
contextual factors and less reference to dispositional factors
than people in the United States (low-context, individualistic) when explaining others' behavior. Similar results emerge
in research on attributions about reasons for promotions and
demotions in organizations in India and the United States
(Smith & Whitehead, 1984), and the use of self-serving biases
in dealing with success and failure experiences in Japan and
the United States (Kashima & Triandis, 1986).

Individuals use the information that they believe is important when interacting with members of other cultures. Because
individuals' explanations are based on their own cultural pre-
suppositions, there is a likelihood misattributions will occur.
Members of low-context cultures, for example, will not emphasize situational factors enough when explaining behavior
of members of high-context cultures. Members of high-context
cultures, in contrast, will not emphasize factors internal to
the individual enough when trying to explain the behavior of
members of low-context cultures.

Another area where misunderstandings may occur in communication between members of low- and high-context cultures is in the directness of speech used. As indicated in
Chapter 3, members of low-context cultures tend to use a direct
style of speech. Members of high-context cultures, in contrast,
tend to use an indirect style of speech. The problems when
people from low- and high-context cultures interact is illustrated in Deborah Tannen's (1979) study of Greek-North American communication.

Tannen (1979) notes that Greeks tend to employ an indirect
style of speech and interpret others' behavior based on the
assumption that they also are using the same style. North
Americans, in contrast, use a direct style of speech and assume
others are using the same style. Tannen observes that when

Greeks and North Americans communicate there often are misunderstandings due to these differences in style of speech. She goes on to point out that overcoming misunderstandings due to direct-indirect style differences is difficult because "in seeking to clarify, each speaker continues to use the very strategy which confused the other in the first place" (p. 5). To resolve the misunderstandings, obviously one of the people involved must recognize that the differences in styles are creating the problem, try to accurately interpret the other person's messages, and then shift her or his style of speech.

Misattributions also result from the way people in low- and high-context cultures try to reduce uncertainty, particularly in initial interactions with strangers. To illustrate, consider how uncertainty is reduced in the United States and Japan. In the white, middle-class subculture in the United States, we try to obtain information about others' attitudes, feelings, and beliefs to reduce our uncertainty. In Japan, on the other hand, people must know others' status and background in order to reduce uncertainty[3] and know which version of the language to use (there are different ways to speak to people who are "superiors," "equals," and "inferiors"). This leads Japanese to introduce themselves saying things like "'I belong to Mitsubishi Bank.' and immediately asking . . . 'What is your job?', 'How old are you?', and 'What is the name of your company?'" (Loveday, 1982, pp. 4-5). These questions are designed to gather the information necessary for a Japanese to communicate with a stranger. They are, however, perceived as "rude" and "nosey" by North Americans.

LEARNING TO MAKE ISOMORPHIC ATTRIBUTIONS

One way we can learn to make isomorphic attributions with a person from another group is through the use of a cultural assimilator. Cultural assimilators are programmed texts that teach us about the other person's culture or ethnic group. In the assimilator, we are provided with a description of a potentially problematic situation. After reading the situation, we are given four possible explanations for the behavior in question and asked to select the response that best explains the situation. If we select the "correct" answer, we are reinforced. If we select a "wrong" answer, we are provided with a reason why the answer we selected is not the best and asked to study the episode again and make another selection.

To illustrate the nature of cultural assimilators, I will use an episode from Slobodin and his associates' (1972) assimilator designed to train white supervisors to work with "hard-core unemployed" black workers. The episode and alternative instructions are as follows (pp. 205-1, 205-2):

> Several hard-core unemployed Blacks had been hired by Jones Tool and Die Company. Mac Grove was one of the supervisors who was supposed to train the Blacks in the procedures of their new jobs. After he had explained the use of one machine, he asked:
>
> "Are there any questions?"
>
> One of the Black workers replied: "Yes, Mr. Grove." At which time Mac interrupted saying: "Oh, call me Mac. Everybody does."
>
> The group moved to another machine and Mac explained its function. He was surprised when one of the other Black workers again addressed him as Mr. Grove.
>
> Why did the Black workers call him Mr. Grove?
>
>   1. They thought Whites in position of authority expect to be called Mr. by Blacks.
>
>   Please go to page 205-3.
>   2. They felt that Mr. was more appropriate under the circumstances.
>
>   Please go to page 205-4.
>   3. They didn't feel comfortable about calling a White by his first name.
>
>   Please go to page 205-5.
>   4. They didn't believe that Mac really wanted to be called Mac. They thought he was just saying the expected thing.
>
>   Please go to page 205-6.

If we selected response 1 and turned to page 205-3, we would see:

> You selected 1: They thought Whites in positions of authority expect to be called Mr. by Blacks.

While this might be true, it doesn't explain why they continued to call him Mr. after he told them to call him Mac.

If we selected response 2 and turned to page 205-4, we would see:

You selected 2: They felt that Mr. was more appropriate under the circumstances.

Yes.

Our data indicate that hard-core unemployed Blacks feel that formal speech indicates mutual respect and provides status. They also feel that establishing this mutual respect indicates friendship and trust. It is a good thing to keep in mind that hard-core Blacks may prefer the more formal use of Mr. until they have established a good relationship with another person. They may prefer to be called Mr. themselves, at first, if the situation is at all formal. Take your cues from Black workers and maintain formality until it seems appropriate to do otherwise.

If we selected response 3 and turned to page 205-5, we would see:

You selected 3: They didn't feel comfortable about calling a White by his first name.

This is not entirely true. Hard-core Blacks call friends, White or Black, by their first names. However, they may have felt uncomfortable about calling the foreman Mac until they got to know him better.

If we selected response 4 and turned to page 205-6, we would see:

You selected 4: They didn't believe that Mac really wanted to be called Mac. They thought he was just saying the expected thing.

This is not the best answer. There is no evidence in the incident to assume this.

After each explanation, except the correct one, readers are instructed to return to the page of the original episode. After the correct response, readers are instructed to turn to page 206 which contains a summary of the points made in a series of related episodes.

Using cultural assimilators is not the only way we can increase the likelihood that we will make appropriate attributions when communicating with people who are different. We can, for example, observe how people from the other culture communicate among themselves or ask questions of people from the other culture. These "skills" are discussed in the next chapter on being perceived as a competent communicator.

Being Perceived as a Competent Communicator

The purpose of this chapter is to look at what it means to be perceived as a competent communicator. I begin by defining communication competence. Following this, I examine the three components of perceived competence: motivation, knowledge, and skills.

❏ Defining Competence

John Wiemann and James Bradac (1989) point out that in everyday usage competence implies "adequate," "sufficient," and/or "suitable." Given this usage, competent communicators are people who "get by" and manage to avoid the "pitfalls" and "traps" of communication.

As pointed out in the previous chapters, misinterpreting others' messages is one of the major pitfalls or traps of the communication process. I, therefore, see effectiveness (i.e., minimizing misunderstandings) as one of the major factors involved in our perceptions of competence. Effectiveness, as I use the term, is related closely to the notions of adequacy and sufficiency in the everyday usage of competence.[1] Suitability implies that our communication is appropriate; we communicate in ways that meet the minimum contextual requirement of the situation in which we find ourselves.

Our specific skills do not ensure that we are perceived as competent in any particular interaction.

There are at least three aspects of the context to which we must pay attention in determining appropriateness:

> (1) The verbal context, that is, making sense in terms of wording, of statements, and of topic; (2) the relationship context, that is, the structuring, type and style of messages so that they are consonant with the particular relationship at hand; and (3) the environmental context, that is, the consideration of constraints imposed on message making by the symbolic and physical environments. (Wiemann & Backlund, 1980, p. 119)

Our perception of competence varies across contexts. Consider former President Reagan. He is perceived as very competent when delivering "canned" speeches (i.e., he is called the "great" communicator). At the same time, he is not perceived as highly competent in answering questions at a news conference extemporaneously.

COMPETENCE AS IMPRESSIONS

Our view of our communication competence may not be the same as that of the person with whom we are communicating. I, for example, might see myself as a very competent communicator and when we interact you may perceive me as not being very competent. An "outside" observer might have still a different perception of my competence. Understanding communication competence, therefore, minimally requires that we take into consideration our own and the other person's perspective.

If we can have different views of our competence than the people with whom we are communicating, then competence is an impression we have of ourselves and others. Stated differently, "competence is not something intrinsic to a person's nature or behavior" (Spitzberg & Cupach, 1984, p. 115). There are several implications of this view of competence:

> First, competence does not actually reside in the performance; it is an *evaluation* of the performance by someone. . . . Second, the fact that *someone* is making the evaluation means that it is subject to error, bias, and judgment inferences; different judges using the same criteria may evaluate the performance differently. Third, since the evaluation always must be made with reference to some set of implicit or explicit *criteria*, the evaluation cannot be understood or validated without knowledge of the criteria being employed; thus, the same performance may be judged to be competent by one standard and incompetent by another. (McFall, 1982, pp. 13-14)

This view of competence clearly suggests that the specific skills we have do not ensure that we are perceived as competent in any particular interaction. Our skills, however, do increase the likelihood that we are able to adapt our behavior so that others see us as competent (Wiemann & Bradac, 1989).

If people from different cultures use the same criteria (e.g., appropriateness) to judge a person's competence, they may still evaluate the same performance differently. Consider the example in the previous chapter of the Japanese asking "How old are you?" during an initial interaction with a North American. Another Japanese observing this interaction would likely evaluate the Japanese speaker's question as appropriate. The North American who is asked the question, in contrast, is likely to see the question as inappropriate.

The standards people use to judge competence also will vary across cultures. Carroll (1988) discusses differences in the way French and North American communicators perceive competency in conversations. The French, for example, tend to value animated conversations in social situations. These conversations are fast-moving with frequent interruptions. Often, the speakers ask questions and do not wait for answers. North Americans, however, prefer fuller answers to questions, less interruptions, and more continuity in the conversation than the French. The French may interpret North American conversation and readiness to discuss serious topics in social gatherings as inappropriate (and incompetent) because more serious conversations occur in contexts other than social situations and require a strong commitment between individuals. While North Americans may view the French style of frequent interruptions and short answers to their questions as inappropriate and, therefore, incompetent.

COMPONENTS OF COMPETENCE

Brian Spitzberg and William Cupach (1984) isolate three components of communication competence: motivation, knowledge, and skills. Motivation refers to our desire to communicate appropriately and effectively with others. Of particular importance to the present analysis is our motivation to communicate with people who are different. Knowledge refers to our awareness or understanding of what needs to be done in order to communicate appropriately and effectively. Skills are our abilities to engage in the behaviors necessary to communicate appropriately and effectively.

We may be highly motivated and lack the knowledge and/ or the skills necessary to communicate appropriately and effectively. We also may be motivated and have the knowledge necessary, but not the skills. If we are motivated and have the knowledge and skills, this does not ensure that we will communicate appropriately or effectively. There are several factors that may intervene to affect our behavior. We may, for example, have a strong emotional reaction to something that happens. Our emotional reaction, in turn, may cause us to "act out" a script we learned earlier in life that is dysfunctional in the situation in which we find ourselves. To illustrate, consider a white, middle-class person from the United States who is served "snake" in another culture. He or she is likely to have a strong negative reaction to eating this meat. If the person is unable to control his or her emotional reaction cognitively, there is little chance that she or he will behave in a way that is perceived as competent by people in the other culture.

It is also possible that the environment may influence our ability to use the knowledge or skills we have. I recently was in Calcutta. While I view my self as a person who can adjust to other cultures relatively easily, the environment in Calcutta affected my ability to use my knowledge and skills. I had such a strong emotional reaction to the poverty I saw (e.g., people searching through garbage for food, large numbers of people sleeping in the street) that initially I was not able to use my knowledge or skills to adapt.

The person with whom we are communicating may also be a factor in our ability to be perceived as competent. If the other person communicates with us in a way that suggests we are not competent, we will, in all likelihood, act in an incompetent fashion.[2] It is also possible that we may act appropriately and effectively without actually having the knowledge necessary to engage in the behaviors by imitating the behavior of another person. While this can work when communicating with people who are different when we do not have sufficient knowledge of the other person's group, it is not the best strategy. I agree with Wiemann and Kelly (1981), "knowledge without skill is socially useless, and skill cannot be obtained without the cognitive ability to diagnose situational demands and constraints" (p. 290).

Our motivation, knowledge, and skills interact with "outcomes" of our interactions with others to yield perceptions of competence. I have mentioned two outcomes—appropriateness and effectiveness—already. Other potential outcomes include, but are not limited to, interpersonal attraction, trust, satisfaction with our communication, the development of inter-personal relationships (i.e., intimacy), resolving conflict, adapting to other cultures, and building community. The remainder of this chapter is devoted to the three components of competence. The final chapter is devoted to applications of these ideas to managing conflict, developing intimate relationships, and building community with strangers.

❑ Motivation

Jonathan H. Turner (1987) suggests that certain basic "needs" motivate us to interact with others. Needs are "fundamental states of being in humans which, if unsatisfied, generate feelings of deprivation" (p. 23). The needs that serve as motivating factors are: (1) our need for a sense of security as a human being, (2) our need for a sense of trust (this need involves issues of predictability; I trust you will behave as I think you will); (3) our need for a sense of group inclusion; (4) our need to avoid diffuse anxiety; (5) our need for a sense of a common shared world; (6) our need for symbolic/material gratification; and (7) our need to sustain our self-conception. These needs vary in the degree to which we are conscious of them. We are the least conscious of the first three, moderately conscious of the fourth, and the most conscious of the last three.

Each of the needs, separately and in combination, influences how we want to present ourselves to others, the intentions we form, and the habits or scripts we follow.[3] The needs also can influence each other. Anxiety, for example, can result from not meeting our needs for group inclusion, trust, security, and/or sustaining our self-concept. J.H. Turner argues that our "overall level of motivational energy" is a function of our level of anxiety produced by these four needs.

MANAGING OUR ANXIETY

While avoiding anxiety is an important motivating factor in our communication with people who are similar, it is critical in our communication with strangers. As indicated in Chapter 4, intergroup anxiety is largely a function of our fear of negative consequences when we interact with people who are different. As our anxiety becomes high, our need for a sense of a common shared world and our need to sustain our self-conception become central (J. H. Turner, 1987). Having a sense of a common shared world and sustaining our self-concept are much more difficult when we communicate with strangers than when we communicate with people who are similar. High anxiety, therefore, leads us to avoid communicating with strangers.

> *Avoiding anxiety and sustaining self-conception leads to an approach-avoidance orientation toward intergroup encounters.*

The combination of our need to avoid anxiety and our need to sustain our self-conception leads to an approach-avoidance orientation toward intergroup encounters.[4] Most of us want to see ourselves as "nonprejudiced" and "caring" people. We may, therefore, want to interact with strangers to sustain our self-concept. At the same time, however, our need to avoid anxiety leads us to want to avoid interactions that are not predictable. Holding both attitudes at the same time is not unusual.

Most us spend the vast majority of our time interacting with people who are relatively similar to us. Our actual contact with people who are different is limited; it is a novel form of interaction (Rose, 1981). If our attempts to communicate with strangers are not successful and we cannot get out of the situations in which we find ourselves easily, then our unconscious need for group inclusion becomes unsatisfied. This leads to anxiety about ourselves and our standing in a group context (J. H. Turner, 1987). The net result is that we retreat into known territory and limit our interactions to people who are similar.

The critical thing that we need to keep in mind is that we can cognitively manage our initial anxiety by increasing our tolerance for ambiguity and/or becoming mindful of our communication. As indicated in Chapter 2, becoming mindful involves the creation of new categories, openness to new information, and awareness of more than one perspective. One way we can create new categories is to look at similarities we share with strangers rather than focusing on the differences. Does the person from the other group, for example, have children who go to the same school as ours? Does he or she belong to the same social clubs we do? Does she or he experience similar frustrations in her or his professional and personal life as we do? Does he or she have similar worries about his or her family as we do? The first two questions search for shared group memberships, while the second two focus on shared values, attitudes, or beliefs.

Robert Bellah, Richard Madsen, William Sullivan, Ann Swidler, and Steven Tipton (1985) point out that we need to seek out commonalities because "with a more explicit understanding of what we have in common and the goals we seek to attain together, the differences between us that remain would be less threatening" (p. 287). Finding commonalities requires that we be mindful of our prejudices. "Racism and sexism and homophobia and religious and cultural intolerance . . . are all ways of denying that other people are the same kind as ourselves" (Brodie, 1989, p. 16).

The position that Bellah and his associates advocate vis-à-vis cultural and/or ethnic differences is consistent with Langer's (1989) contention that

> because most of us grow up and spend our time with people like ourselves, we tend to assume uniformities and commonalities. When confronted with someone who is clearly different in one specific way, we drop that assumption and look for differences. . . . The mindful curiosity generated by an encounter with someone

who is different, which can lead to exaggerated perceptions of strangeness, can also bring us closer to that person if channeled differently. (p. 156)

Langer's research suggests that once individuals satisfy their curiosity about differences, understanding can occur. She, therefore, argues that what is needed is a way to make mindful curiosity about differences not taboo. One way that each of us can contribute to the acceptance of mindful curiosity is by interpreting others' questions about us and our groups as "requests for information" until we are certain there is another motivation.

We also can become open to new information by modifying our expectations. If, for example, we have an inflexible negative stereotype of another group, we can either modify the content of the stereotype or hold it more flexibly. We can consciously recognize that our stereotype may be inaccurate and does not apply to *all*, or even most, members of the other group.

We can be mindful of the fact that strangers have different interpretations of what is happening than we do. Understanding their perspectives requires knowledge of their group and the unique perspective they bring to our interaction. The bottom line is that if we become mindful, manage our anxiety, and interact with strangers, we may find out that we actually enjoy communicating with them.

ASSESSING YOUR APPROACH-AVOIDANCE ORIENTATION

The questionnaire in Table 6.1 is designed to help you assess your tendency to approach or avoid interacting with strangers. Take a few minutes to complete it now.

Scores on the questionnaire range from 5 to 25. The higher your score, the greater your tendency to approach strangers. The important thing to remember is that if your score is "low," you can consciously manage your anxiety and change your tendency, if you want to change it.

Table 6.1 Assessing Your Approach-Avoidance Tendencies

The purpose of this questionnaire is to help you assess your tendency to approach or avoid contact with strangers. Respond to each of the statements by indicating the degree to which the statement is true regarding how you typically think about yourself. When you think about yourself, is the statement "Always False" (answer 1), "Usually False" (answer 2), "Sometimes True and Sometimes False" (answer 3), "Usually True" (answer 4), or "Always True (answer 5)?

_____ 1. I have the opportunity to meet people who are different regularly.

_____ 2. I try to encourage social relations with people who are different.

_____ 3. I think close relations with people who are different is desirable.

_____ 4. I have tried to develop friendships with people who are different.

_____ 5. I would not object if someone in my family married a person who is different from us.

To find your score, add the numbers you wrote next to each statement. Scores will range from 5 to 25. The higher your score, the more willing you are to approach people who are different.

SOURCE: Some of the items on this questionnaire are adapted from Hofman (1985).

❑ Knowledge

The knowledge component of communication competence refers to our awareness of what we need to do to communicate in an appropriate and effective way. This includes a specific awareness of the "skills" discussed in the next section and how they can be used when communicating with strangers. When communicating with strangers, we also need to have knowledge about the other person's group. My focus is this section, therefore, is on how we can gather information about strangers and their groups so that we can interpret their messages accurately. While my focus is on gathering information about strangers, the processes outlined apply equally to gathering information about people who are similar.

INFORMATION SEEKING STRATEGIES

Charles Berger (1979) isolated three general types of strategies we can use to gather information about others and reduce our uncertainty about them and the way they will interact with us: passive, active, and interactive strategies. When we use passive strategies we take the role of "unobtrusive observers" (i.e., we do not intervene in the situation we are observing). To illustrate this process, assume that we want to find out about Yoko, a Japanese to whom we have just been introduced.

Obviously, the type of situation in which we observe Yoko influences the amount of information we gain about her. If we observe Yoko in a situation where she does not have to interact with others, we will not gain much information about her. Situations in which she is interacting with several people at once, in contrast, allow us to make comparisons of how Yoko interacts with the different people.

If we know any of the people with whom Yoko is interacting, we can compare how Yoko interacts with the people we know and how she might interact with us. It also should be noted that if other Japanese are present in the situation, we can compare Yoko's behavior with theirs to try to determine how she is similar to and different from other Japanese.

There is one other aspect of the situation that will influence the amount of information we obtain about Yoko's behavior. If the situation is a formal one, her behavior is likely to be a function of the role she is filling in the situation and we will not learn much about Yoko as an individual. Situations where behavior is not guided by roles or social protocol, on the other hand, will provide useful information on Yoko's behavior.

The preceding examples all involve our taking the role of an observer. The active strategies for reducing uncertainty require us to do something to acquire information about Yoko. One thing we could do to get information about Yoko is to ask questions of someone who knows her. When we ask others about someone we need to keep in mind that the information we receive may not be accurate. The other person may intentionally give us wrong information or the other person may not really know Yoko well.

We can also gather information about other groups by asking people who have had contact with those groups or gathering information from the library. In this example, we could gather information on Japan by questioning someone we know who has lived in Japan, reading a book on Japanese culture, or completing a Japanese cultural assimilator (discussed in the preceding chapter). This would give us information about Yoko's cultural background that would allow us to make cultural level predictions about her behavior. Again, we need to keep in mind that our informant may or may not have good information about Japan and that Yoko may not be a typical Japanese.

This raises the issue of how we can select good informants to learn about other groups. People who have a lot of informal social contact with members of the other group, for example, are better informants than people who have little informal contact or even a lot of contact in formal settings. We also would be well off to select informants who have been successful in their interactions with members of other groups. To illustrate, if there are two members of our group who have frequent contact with the group in which we are interested, we would select the one who appears to be most successful in interacting with members of the other group (based on our observations of their interactions or their reports of their interactions).

When we use active strategies to gather information we do not actually interact with the people about whom we are trying to gather information. The interactive strategies of verbal interrogation (question asking) and self-disclosure, in contrast, are used when we interact with the other person.

One obvious way we can gather information about others is to ask them questions. When we are interacting with someone who is similar, there are limitations to this strategy that have to be kept in mind. First, we can ask only so many questions. I am not sure of what the number is, but I always know when

I have asked too many. Second, our questions must be appropriate to the nature of the interaction we are having and the relationship we have with the other person.

When we are communicating with strangers, the same limitations are present, and there are others. The number and type of questions that strangers consider acceptable may not be the same as what we consider acceptable (recall the example of the questions the Japanese asked in the previous chapter). Strangers also may not be able to answer our questions, especially if our questions deal with why they behave the way they do [the ultimate answer to why questions is "because!" (that is the way we do it here)]. When interacting with strangers there is also the added problem of our not wanting to appear "stupid" or be "rude." We, therefore, often avoid asking questions of strangers.

If we can overcome our fear of looking "stupid," asking questions is an excellent way to gather information about strangers. Generally speaking, strangers will probably respond in a positive way as long as they perceive that our intent is to learn about them personally or their group and *not* to judge them.[5]

The other way we can gather information about another person when interacting with her or him is through self-disclosure—telling the other person unknown information about ourselves.[6] Self-disclosure works as an information gathering strategy because of the reciprocity norm.[7] Essentially, the reciprocity norm states that if I do something for you, you will reciprocate and do something for me. The reciprocity norm appears to be a cultural universal; it exists in all cultures.[8]

In conversations between people who are not close (i.e., people we meet for the first time, acquaintances), we tend to reciprocate and tell each other the same information about ourselves that the other person tells us. If I disclose my opinion on a topic when we are talking, you will probably tell me your opinion on the same topic. There will, however, be some differences when we communicate with strangers than when we communicate with people from our own group. The topics that are appropriate to be discussed, for example, vary from culture to culture and ethnic group to ethnic group. If we self-disclose on a topic with a stranger and she or he does not reciprocate, there is a good chance we have found an inappropriate topic of conversation in that person's group. Because the timing and pacing of self-disclosure varies across cultures and ethnic groups, it is also possible that our timing is off or we have tried to self-disclose at an inappropriate pace.

To summarize, there are some general "steps" we can follow to try to better understand how people who are different interpret our interactions with them. If we apply these steps, our knowledge of people who are different should increase.

(1) After we have an experience with a person who is different, we need to stop and observe what we have experienced. *Describe* what we saw happening. As indicated in Chapter 1, description is a report of what we observed with the minimum of distortion and without attributing social significance (i.e., meaning).

(2) Look for *alternative interpretations* (i.e., the social significance or meaning) of what we described. Try to figure out how the other person is interpreting what occurred; what did it mean to him or her.

(3) If we are unable to guess how the other person is interpreting what happened with a high degree of confidence, we need to seek additional information—use the information gathering strategies outlined above (e.g., go to the library and find information on the other group, ask the other person, ask someone from his or her group, ask someone from our group who has had extensive experience with people from the other group, etc.).

(4) After we have obtained additional information, we need to draw a conclusion as to how we think the other person is interpreting what happened. Given our understanding of what happened, we can then *evaluate* what happened. Do we like it or dislike it, given our understanding of how the other person interpreted it?

(5) Incorporate our conclusions into our understanding of the other person and/or group. We must remember, however,

that our conclusions and understanding may be inaccurate and not generalize to all people in the other group.

It often is not necessary to go through all five steps. If we have some knowledge of the other person and his or her group, we usually can make a reasonable guess as to how she or he is interpreting what is going on when we are mindful of our communication. Step 3, therefore, can be omitted. Processing our interpretations mindfully in this way does take longer than responding mindlessly, but the time it takes results in greater effectiveness.

ASSESSING YOUR KNOWLEDGE OF ANOTHER GROUP

Table 6.2 contains a questionnaire designed to help you assess your knowledge about another group. To complete the questionnaire you need to think of a specific group (e.g., another culture or ethnic group). Take a couple of minutes to complete the questionnaire now.

Scores on the questionnaire range from 5 to 25. The higher your score, the greater your understanding of the other group. The thing to keep in mind is that the higher your score, the less likely you will misinterpret messages you receive from members of this group.

UNCERTAINTY ORIENTATION

There is one cognitive/affective process, uncertainty orientation, that appears to influence whether or not we try to gather information about others that needs to be discussed before addressing skills. Richard Sorrentino and Judith-Ann Short (1986) point out

that there are many people who simply are not interested in finding out information about themselves or the world, who do not conduct causal searches, who could not care less about comparing themselves with others, and who "don't give a hoot" for resolving discrepancies or inconsistencies about the self. Indeed, such people (we call them certainty oriented) will go out of their

Table 6.2 Assessing Your Knowledge of Another Group

The purpose of this questionnaire is to help you assess your knowledge of another culture or ethnic group. The statements in this questionnaire contain a blank space. Think of a specific culture or ethnic group when you are reading the statements. Respond to each statement by indicating the degree to which the statement is true regarding your knowledge: "Always False" (answer 1), "Usually False" (answer 2), "Sometimes True and Sometimes False" (answer 3), "Usually True" (answer 4), or "Always True" (answer 5).

1. I understand the norms of _____ .

2. I understand the customs of _____ .

3. I understand the values of _____ .

4. I understand the communication rules of _____ .

5. I understand the language (or dialect) of _____ .

To find your score, add the numbers your wrote next to each statement. Scores range from 5 to 25. The higher your score, the greater your knowledge of the group.

way not to perform activities such as these (we call people who *do* go out of their way to do such things uncertainty oriented). (pp. 379-380)

Uncertainty oriented people integrate new and old ideas and change their belief systems accordingly.[9] They evaluate ideas and thoughts on their own merit and do not necessarily compare them with others. Uncertainty oriented people want to understand themselves and their environment. Certainty oriented people, in contrast, like to hold on to traditional beliefs and have a tendency to reject ideas that are different. Certainty oriented people maintain a sense of self by not examining themselves or their behavior.

The more uncertainty oriented we are, the more likely we are willing to question our own behavior and its appropriateness when communicating with strangers. Also, the more uncertainty oriented we are, the more we would try to gather information about strangers so we can communicate effectively with them.

If you are reading this book by choice and have gotten this far, you probably are relatively uncertainty oriented (this may not hold if you are reading it for a class and are going to be tested over it). The questionnaire in Table 6.3 is designed to help you assess your certainty-uncertainty orientation. Take a few minutes and complete it now.

Scores on the questionnaire range from 5 to 25. The higher your score, the more uncertainty oriented you are. The thing to keep in mind is that the less uncertainty oriented you are (or the more certainty oriented you are), the greater the potential misunderstandings you may have when you communicate with people who are different. If you are highly certainty oriented (i.e., you got a low score on the questionnaire), you have a lot of misunderstandings and may not know about them or care about them if you do recognize them. While Sorrentino and Short talk about uncertainty orientation as a "personality" trait, I believe our orientation can be "managed," at least in part, if we are mindful when we communicate.

❏ Skills

The skills necessary to communicate effectively and appropriately with strangers are those that are directly related to reducing our uncertainty and anxiety.[9] Reducing and/or controlling our anxiety requires at least two skills: becoming mindful and developing a tolerance for ambiguity. Reducing uncertainty minimally requires three skills: empathy, behavioral flexibility, and the ability to reduce uncertainty itself (the first two skills, however, are necessary to develop the third).

BECOMING MINDFUL

By now, it should be clear that I believe becoming mindful is an important aspect of communicating effectively with strangers. We must be cognitively aware of our communication if we

Table 6.3 Assessing Your Uncertainty Orientation

The purpose of this questionnaire is to help you assess your orientation toward uncertainty. Respond to each statement indicating the degree to which it is true regarding the way to typically respond: "Always False" (answer 1), "Usually False" (answer 2), "Sometimes False and Sometimes True" (answer 3), "Usually True" (answer 4), or "Always True" (answer 5).

_____ 1. When I obtain new information, I try to integrate it with information I already have.

_____ 2. If given a choice, I prefer to go somewhere new rather than somewhere I've been before.

_____ 3. I evaluate people on their own merit without comparing them to others.

_____ 4. I try to resolve inconsistencies in beliefs I hold.

_____ 5. If someone suggests an opinion that is different than mine, I do not reject it before I consider it.

To find your score, add the numbers you wrote next to each statement. Scores range from 5 to 25. The higher your score, the greater your uncertainty orientation.

SOURCE: The statements on this questionnaire were developed based on Sorrentino and Short's (1986) description of certainty and uncertainty orientations.

are to overcome our tendency to interpret strangers' behavior based on our own system. Because I have talked about mindfulness at length throughout the book, I will not go into great detail here. There is, however, one point I want to reiterate. Namely, we are seldom highly mindful of our communication.

When we interact with strangers, we do become somewhat mindful of our communication. Our focus, however, is usually on the outcome ("Will I make a fool of myself?"), rather than the process of communication. Even when we communicate with people close to us, we are not mindful of the process. Mihaly Csikszentmihalyi (1990) contends that

> there are few things as enjoyable as freely sharing one's most secret feelings and thoughts with another person. Even though this sounds commonplace, it in fact requires concentrated attention

[mindfulness], openness, and sensitivity. In practice, the degree of investment of psychic energy in a friendship is unfortunately rare. (p. 188)

He goes on to argue that we must "control" our own lives if we want to improve our relationships with others. Such control requires that we be mindful.

The questionnaire in Table 6.4 is designed to help you assess how mindful you are when you communicate. This is a difficult idea to assess. To complete the questionnaire you must think about your communication (i.e., become mindful of it). This will lead you to overestimate how mindful you actually are when you communicate. The questionnaire, nevertheless, will give you a rough idea of where you fall with respect to being mindful if you try to answer the questions based on your "normal" patterns of communication. Take a few minutes to complete it now.

Scores on the questionnaire range from 5 to 25. The higher your score, the more mindful you are when you communicate. Keep in mind that your score probably is inflated because you were mindful when you completed the questionnaire. Also remember that mindfulness is a skill that we can manage. If your score is low, you can train yourself to be more mindful about your communication. One way to accomplish this is to complete the exercises in a book (e.g., Beck, 1988) on cognitive therapy.

TOLERANCE FOR AMBIGUITY

Tolerance for ambiguity implies the ability to deal success-fully with situations, even when a lot of information needed to interact effectively is unknown. Brent Ruben and Daniel Kealey (1979) point out that

the ability to react to new and ambiguous situations with mini-mal discomfort has long been thought to be an important asset

Table 6.4 Assessing Your Ability to Be Mindful

The purpose of this questionnaire is to help you assess your ability to be mindful when you communicate. Respond to each statement by indicating the degree to which it is true regarding the way you normally communicate: "Always False" (answer 1), "Usually False" (answer 2), "Sometimes False and Sometimes True" (answer 3), "Usually True" (answer 4), or "Always True" (answer 5).

_____ 1. I pay attention to the situation and context when I communicate.

_____ 2. I can describe others with whom I communicate in great detail.

_____ 3. I seek out new information about the people with whom I communicate.

_____ 4. I try to find rational reasons why others may behave in a way I perceive negatively.

_____ 5. I recognize that the person with whom I am communicating has a different point of view than I do.

To find your score, add the numbers you wrote next to each statement. Scores range from 5 to 25. The higher your score, the more mindful you are when you communicate.

SOURCE: The statements on this questionnaire are drawn from Langer's (1989) description of mindfulness.

> when adjusting to a new culture. . . . Excessive discomfort result-
> ing from being placed in a new or different environment—or from
> finding the familiar environment altered in some critical ways—
> can lead to confusion, frustration and interpersonal hostility. Some
> people seem better able to adapt well in new environments and
> adjust quickly to the demands of the changing milieu. (p. 19)

Ruben and Kealey's research indicates that the greater our tolerance for ambiguity, the more effective we are in completing task assignments in other cultures.

Our tolerance for ambiguity affects the type of information we try to find out about others. People with a low tolerance for ambiguity try to gather information that supports their own beliefs. People with a high tolerance for ambiguity, in contrast, seek "objective" information from others (McPherson, 1983). Objective information is necessary to understand strangers and accurately predict their behavior.

Table 6.5 Assessing Your Tolerance for Ambiguity

The purpose of this questionnaire is to help you assess your orientations toward ambiguity. Respond to each statement indicating the degree to which it is true regarding the way you typically respond: "Always False" (answer 1), "Usually False" (answer 2), "Sometimes False and Sometimes True" (answer 3), "Usually True" (answer 4), or "Always True" (answer 5).

_____ 1. I am comfortable in new situations.

_____ 2. I deal with unforeseen problems successfully.

_____ 3. I experience little discomfort in ambiguous situations.

_____ 4. I am relaxed in unfamiliar situations.

_____ 5. I am not frustrated when things do not go the way I expected.

To find your score, add the numbers you wrote next to each statement. Scores range from 5 to 25. The higher your score, the greater your tolerance for ambiguity.

The questionnaire in Table 6.5 is designed to help you assess your tolerance for ambiguity. Take a couple of minutes and complete it now.

Scores on the questionnaire range from 5 to 25. The higher your score, the greater your tolerance for ambiguity.

EMPATHY

The one skill that consistently emerges in discussions of competence in communicating with strangers is empathy. To understand empathy, we need to contrast it with sympathy. Sympathy refers to "the imaginative placing of ourselves in another person's position" (Bennett, 1979, p. 411). When we sympathize we use our own frame of reference to try to figure out how the other person is feeling. Milton Bennett (1979) argues that if we apply the Golden Rule ("Do unto others as you would have them do unto you") when communicating with strangers, we are being sympathetic because the referent is our own standard of appropriate behavior.

In contrast to sympathy, empathy is "the imaginative intellectual and emotional participation in another person's experience" (Bennett, 1979, p. 418). The referent for interpreting

Table 6.6 Assessing Your Empathy

The purpose of this questionnaire is to help you assess your ability to empathize. Respond to each statement by indicating the degree to which the statement is true regarding the way you typically communicate with others. When you think of your communication, is the statement "Always False" (answer 1), "Usually False" (answer 2), "Sometimes False and Sometimes True" (answer 3), "Usually True" (answer 4), or "Always True" (answer 5).

_____ 1. I try to understand others' experiences from their perspectives.

_____ 2. When others are having problems, I can imagine how they feel.

_____ 3. I can "tune in" to the emotions others are experiencing when we communicate.

_____ 4. I try to see others as they want me to.

_____ 5. I am able to tell what others are feeling without being told.

To find your score, add the numbers you wrote next to each statement. Scores range from 5 to 25. The higher your score, the more you are able to empathize.

the experience is not our own, but rather the other person's. Bennett proposes that we substitute the "Platinum Rule" ("Do unto others as they themselves would have done unto them"; p. 422) for the Golden Rule. This is a reasonable approach as long as what others want done unto them does not violate our basic moral principles or universally accepted principles of human rights.[10]

Table 6.6 contains a questionnaire designed to help you assess your ability to display empathy. Take a few minutes to complete it now.

Scores on the questionnaire range from 5 to 25. The higher your score, the greater your empathy. If your score is on the low side, remember that you can increase your tendency to display empathy when you are mindful of your communication.

BEHAVIORAL FLEXIBILITY

To gather information about and adapt our behavior to strangers requires that we are flexible in our behavior.[11] As suggested in the discussion of knowledge, we must be able to select strategies that are appropriate to gather the information we need about strangers in order to communicate effectively with them. This requires that we have different behavioral options open to us. Do I sit back and watch the other person or go interact with him or her? Which strategy will provide the information I need to know to communicate effectively?

We also must be able to adapt and accommodate our behavior to people from other groups if we are going to be successful in our interactions with them. One important aspect of adapting our behavior is the ability to speak another language (or at least use phrases in another language). If we always expect strangers to speak our language, we cannot be effective in communicating with them. Ernest Boyer (1990), Chair of the Carnegie Endowment for Teaching, points out that we "should become familiar with other languages and cultures so that [we] will be better able to live, with confidence, in an increasingly interdependent world" (p. B4).

Harry Triandis (1983) points out that the importance of speaking another language depends, at least in part, on where you are:

> In some cultures foreigners are expected to know the local language. A Frenchman [or woman] who arrives in the United States without knowing a word of English, or an American who visits France with only a bit of French, is bound to find the locals rather unsympathetic. For example, I have found a discrepancy between my friends' and my own experience in Paris. Their accounts stress discourtesy of the French while I have found the French to be quite courteous. I suspect the difference is that I speak better French than the majority of visitors and am therefore treated more courteously. In contrast, in other cultures the visitor is not expected to know the local language. In Greece, for example, one is not expected to know the language although a few words of Greek can create delight, and increase by order of magnitude (a factor of ten) the normal hospitable tendencies of that population. (p. 84)

Some attempt at using the local language is necessary to indicate an interest in the people and/or culture.

The need to adapt our behavior is not limited to speaking another language. If I (a white male from the United States) am communicating with someone from another culture who wants to stand much closer to me than I want him or her to stand (e.g., someone from a Latin or Arab culture), I have two options if I am mindful of my communication.

First, I can choose to try to use my own interpersonal distance (e.g., the other person should stand at least at arm's length from me). If the other person keeps trying to use her or his distance, however, he or she will "dance" me around the room (i.e., the other person moves forward, I move back; to compensate and be at a distance that is comfortable for him or her, the other person moves closer). If I am not mindful of my communication, this is what is likely to occur.

Alternatively, I can choose to use a different pattern of behavior. I can decide to stand closer to the other person than I would if I was communicating with someone from my own culture. This option will, in all likelihood, lead to more effective communication. When people are following different norms, at least one of the parties has to adapt for effective communication to occur.

You may be thinking, why should I have to adapt? Why doesn't the other person adapt, especially if he or she is a foreigner in the United States? The other person could adapt, and people from other cultures visiting or living in the United States usually do to some extent. I believe, however, that as members of the human community we have to make choices about whether to adapt and when to adapt to others.

In commenting on a draft of this book, Harry Triandis (personal communication, September 4, 1990) pointed out that being flexible is part of being educated. He argues that flexibility "means that you have more doors open to you (jobs, countries). It means being able to adjust to more situations. So multicultural skills . . . are an essential element of being educated."

My position is that if we know what can be done to improve the chances for effective communication, have the skills to do what needs to be done, and choose not to adapt, we must take responsibility for misunderstandings that occur as a result. There are obviously situations where this principle may not hold. If the behavior required, for example, goes against my moral standards or violates another's human rights, some other option must be found.

The questionnaire in Table 6.7 is designed to help you to assess your behavioral flexibility. The questionnaire obviously does not tap all aspects of how we might be flexible. It does, however, cover the major areas needed to communicate effectively with people who are different. Take a few minutes to complete it now.

Scores on the questionnaire range from 5 to 25. The higher your score, the more flexible you are in your behavioral repertoire. The important thing to keep in mind if you do not have a high score is that you can increase your behavioral flexibility with practice. Once you understand what behavior is necessary (i.e., have the necessary knowledge) become mindful of your communication, and try out the behavior. Who knows, you may find that you like it.

ABILITY TO REDUCE UNCERTAINTY

The final skill to be discussed is the ability to reduce uncertainty itself. If you can empathize and have behavioral flexibility, you can gather the information necessary to reduce uncertainty. As indicated earlier, reducing uncertainty requires that we be able to describe others' behavior, select accurate interpretations of their messages, accurately predict their behavior, and be able to explain their behavior. When we also are controlling our anxiety, these abilities should lead to appropriate and effective communication.

The questionnaire in Table 6.8 is designed to help you assess your ability to reduce uncertainty with people who are different when you communicate with them. Take a couple of minutes and complete the questionnaire now.

Table 6.7 Assessing Your Behavioral Flexibility

The purpose of this questionnaire is to help you assess the flexibility in your patterns of behavior. Respond to each statement by indicating the extent to which it is true of your normal patterns of communication: "Always False" (answer 1), "Usually False" (answer 2), "Sometimes False and Sometimes True" (answer 3), "Usually True" (answer 4), or "Always True" (answer 5).

_____ 1. I adapt my behavior to the person with whom I am communicating.

_____ 2. I am able to modify how I present myself to others.

_____ 3. I adapt my behavior to the situation in which I find myself once I know what behavior is required.

_____ 4. I can modify the way I come across to people, depending on the impression I want to give them.

_____ 5. I communicate differently with acquaintances and with close friends.

To find your score, add the numbers you wrote next to each statement. Scores range from 5 to 25. The higher your score, the greater your behavioral flexibility.

SOURCE: The ideas for several of these statements were taken from Lennox and Wolfe's (1984) ability to modify self-presentations scale.

The scores on the questionnaire range from 5 to 25. The higher your score, the greater your understanding of people who are different. The greater your understanding of people who are different, the more effective your communication will be.

The questionnaire in Table 6.8 is designed to assess your "general" ability to reduce uncertainty with people who are different. You also can use the questions to assess your ability to reduce uncertainty with respect to a specific group (substitute the group for "people who are different" in each statement) or a specific person (substitute the person's name for "people who are different" in each statement). You would interpret these scores in the same way as your general score. The higher your score, the less the likelihood of misunderstandings when you communicate.

To conclude, this chapter has been devoted to looking at the factors that contribute to our being perceived as a competent

Table 6.8 Assessing Your Ability to Reduce Uncertainty

The purpose of this questionnaire is to help you assess your ability to reduce uncertainty when communicating with people who are different. Respond to each statement by indicating the degree to which the statement is true with respect to your communication with people who are different. When you communicate with people who are different, is the statement "Always False" (answer 1), "Usually False" (answer 2), "Sometimes True and Sometimes False" (answer 3), "Usually True" (answer 4), or "Always True" (answer 5).

_____ 1. I can make accurate predictions regarding the behavior of people who are different.

_____ 2. I generally understand the behavior of people who are different.

_____ 3. I can explain the behavior of people who are different to others.

_____ 4. I can accurately interpret the behavior of people who are different.

_____ 5. I can accurately describe the behavior of people who are different.

To find your score, add the numbers you wrote next to each of the statements. Scores range from 5 to 25. The higher your score, the greater your understanding of people who are different.

communicator—our motivation, knowledge, and skills. In the final chapter, I apply these ideas to managing conflict, developing relationships, and building community with strangers.

Applying Our Knowledge and Skills

I examined the factors that contribute to perceptions of our competence in communicating with strangers in the preceding chapter. In this chapter, I discuss three areas in which we can apply our knowledge and skills. I begin by looking at how we can manage conflict with strangers constructively. Next, I examine how we develop intimate relationships with strangers. I then discuss how we can apply our knowledge and skills for resolving conflict and developing interpersonal relationships to building community with strangers.

❏ Resolving Conflict

Conflict is inevitable in any relationship, it is going to happen whether we want it to or not. Many of us, nevertheless, view conflict negatively. Conflict itself, however, is not positive or negative. How we manage the conflicts we have, in contrast, can have positive or negative consequences for our relationships.

Kenneth Thomas (1983) defines dyadic conflict as "the process which begins when one party perceives that the other has frustrated, or is about to frustrate, some concern of his" or hers (p. 891). This definition covers a broad range of phenomena. Conflicts can arise from instrumental (i.e., differences in goals or practices) or expressive (i.e., tension, often generated from hostile feelings) sources (Olsen, 1978).

CULTURAL AND ETHNIC DIFFERENCES IN CONFLICT

Instrumental and expressive conflicts arise in all cultures. There are, however, cultural differences in the sources people tend to perceive as the major "cause" of conflict. People in low-context, individualistic cultures, for example, usually interpret the source of conflicts as being instrumental in nature. Because the conflict is instrumentally based, people can argue over task-oriented issues and remain friends. People in high-context, collectivistic cultures, in contrast, tend to see conflict arising from expressive sources (Ting-Toomey, 1985). Because the person and the issue are not separated, it is difficult to have open disagreement without one or both parties losing face.

Stella Ting-Toomey (1988) argues that individualism-collectivism can be used to explain preferred conflict styles across cultures. She suggests that people in individualistic cultures prefer direct styles of dealing with conflict such as dominating, controlling, and/or solution-orientation. People in collectivistic cultures, on the other hand, prefer indirect styles of dealing with conflict that allow all parties to preserve face. They tend to use obliging and smoothing styles of conflict resolution or avoid the conflict altogether. These differences are consistent with Dean Barnlund's (1975) description of conflict strategies in Japan and the United States. He suggests that people in the United States

prefer to defend themselves actively, employing or developing the
rationale for positions they have taken. When pushed they may
resort to still more aggressive forms that utilize humor, sarcasm,
or denunciation. Among Japanese, the reactions are more varied,
but defenses tend to be more passive, permit withdrawal, and
allow greater concealment. (p. 423)

Avoiding conflict in order to preserve face is not limited to
the Japanese culture. A study of Chinese and North Americans,
for example, revealed that Chinese would advise an executive
to meet with an insulter and the target of the insult separately
so that conflict between the two can be avoided. People in the
United States, in contrast, would advise an executive to have a
joint meeting so that the problem between the insulter and
target of the insult can be resolved (Bond, Wan, Leung, &
Giacalone, 1985). Similar differences emerge when people in
the United States and Mexico are compared. Specifically, Mex-
icans tend to avoid or deny that conflict exists, while people in
the United States tend to use direct strategies to deal with it
(e.g., McGinn, Harburg, & Ginsburg, 1973).[1]

Most, if not all, of the cross-cultural studies comparing the
United States with other cultures have focused on Caucasians.
It must be noted that there also are differences across ethnic
groups in the United States.[2] Ting-Toomey (1986), for example, found that blacks prefer a controlling conflict resolution
style, while whites prefer a solution-oriented style. Thomas
Kochman's (1981) descriptions of black and white styles of
communication are consistent with these findings. He points
out that

where whites use the relatively detached and unemotional *discussion* mode to engage an issue, blacks use the more emotionally
intense and involving mode of *argument*. Where whites tend to
underestimate their exceptional talents and abilities, blacks tend to
boast about theirs. (p. 106)

Kochman goes on to observe that blacks favor "forceful" outputs (e.g., volume of voice), while whites prefer "subdued"

outputs. Blacks interpret whites subdued responses as "life-less" and whites interpret blacks' responses as in "bad taste."

Kochman isolates several other areas where whites' and blacks' styles of communication may be problematic when they communicate with each other, particularly in a conflict situation. One area of importance for dealing with conflict is how members of the two groups view their responsibilities to the others' sensibilities and feelings. He illustrates differences in this area by discussing differences in reactions to an assignment he gave in an interpersonal communication class. Students in the class were told to "confront" each other and comment on their perceptions of each others' style of communication. The student responses to the assignment divided basically along ethnic lines:

> Twelve of the fourteen white students argued for the right of students *not* to hear what others might want to say about them— thus giving priority to the protection of individual sensibilities, those of others as well as their own, even if this might result in forfeiting their own chance to say what they felt. . . . The eight black students and the remaining two white students, on the other hand, argued for the rights of those students to express what they had to say about others even if the protection of all individual sensibilities would be forfeited in the process. On this last point, one black woman said: "I don't know about others, but if someone has something to say to me, I want to hear it." (pp. 122-123)

Kochman argues that withdrawing the protection of sensibilities is seen as "insensitive" or "cruel" by whites, while blacks see whites failing to say what they think as lack of concern for their "real" selves.

One of the major implications of these differences is what happens when blacks and whites are involved in a conflict situation. Kochman points out that "the greater capacity of blacks to express themselves forcefully and to receive and manipulate the forceful assertions of others gives them greater leverage in interracial encounters" (p. 126). When blacks offend whites' social sensibilities, whites demand an apology. Blacks see this demand as "weak" and "inappropriate." Part of the difference is in who is considered responsible when people are upset. When whites are upset, they tend to see the cause as the other person. Blacks, in contrast, see themselves as responsible for their feelings. "Blacks will commonly say to those who have become angry, '*Others* did not make you angry'; rather, 'You *let yourself* become angry'" (Kochman, 1981, p. 127).

The preceding examples are designed only to illustrate the cultural and ethnic differences in the approaches to conflict. It is important to keep in mind, however, that there are differences within ethnic groups. Responses to Kochman's class assignment, for example, illustrated that some whites share the approach of his black students. In conflict situations, it is important to be aware of *potential* cultural or ethnic differences in the approach to conflict, but the focus in resolving the conflict has to be on being mindful of our communication and dealing with the other person as an individual.

MANAGING CONFLICT

As indicated earlier, it is not conflict per se that is positive or negative. How we manage the conflict, however, can have positive or negative consequences for our relationships. In managing conflict with strangers, or with people who are similar, it is important that we establish what Jack Gibb (1961) calls a "supportive climate."

The first characteristic of a supportive climate is description rather than evaluation. We cannot understand others if we evaluate them before we understand their positions. Using evaluative speech brings up our defenses. Descriptive speech, in contrast, does not make the other person uneasy and, in addition, it allows us to find out how they are interpreting what is happening.

Taking a problem orientation is the second characteristic of a supportive climate. Defining a "mutual problem" and expressing a willingness to collaborate in finding a solution implies that we have no predetermined outcome we want to see. If we have a predetermined outcome in mind and try to "force" this outcome on the other person, we are trying to "control" them. Attempts to control others are inevitably met with resistance.

Being spontaneous, as opposed to being strategic, is the third characteristic of a supportive climate. If I appear to have a hidden motive and am acting in what appears a strategic way to you, it will arouse defensiveness in you. If you appear spontaneous and not strategic to me, on the other hand, I will not get defensive.

> *Always be unconditionally constructive.*

Empathy also is important in establishing a supportive environment. As indicated in the previous chapter, if I convey empathy in my communication with you, you will know that I am concerned with your welfare. If you appear "neutral" toward me, I will become defensive.

The fifth characteristic of a supportive climate is communicating that we are equal. If I talk in a way that you perceive as "sounding superior," you will become defensive. If we truly want to manage conflicts with strangers, we must avoid communicating at Lukens' distances of indifference, avoidance, and disparagement, and communicate at a distance of sensitivity or equality.

The final characteristic of a supportive climate is "provisionalism." If I communicate to you that I am open to your viewpoint and willing to "experiment" with my behavior (i.e., try to change it if needed), you will not become defensive. If, on the other hand, I communicate in such a way that indicates that I think I am right and "certain" of my attitudes and behavior, you will become defensive.

Many of these characteristics of a supportive climate should sound familiar. While the words are not exactly the same, the attitude Gibb suggests in order to resolve conflict is very similar to Langer's notion of becoming mindful. In becoming mindful, we have to create new categories (which is necessary to be descriptive), be open to new information, and not be "certain" that we already know the answers. The focus is on the process, not the outcome.

Roger Fisher and Scott Brown (1988) of the Harvard Negotiation Project recommend a similar approach for conducting negotiations. They begin with the assumption that one participant can change a relationship. If we change the way we react to others, they will change the way they react to us. The objective of change is developing "a relationship that can deal with differences" (p. 3). Achieving change requires that we separate relationship and substantive issues and pursue goals in each arena separately.

Fisher and Brown offer a prescriptive approach to effective negotiations. Stated most simply they believe that we should always be unconditionally constructive. They contend we must:

> Do only those things that are both good for the relationship and good for us, whether or not they reciprocate.
>
> 1. Rationality. Even if they are acting emotionally, balance emotion with reason.
> 2. Understanding. Even if they misunderstand us, try to understand them.
> 3. Communication. Even if they are not listening, consult them before deciding on matters that affect them.
> 4. Reliability. Even if they are trying to deceive us, neither trust nor deceive them; be reliable.
> 5. Noncoercive modes of influence. Even if they are trying to coerce us, neither yield to that coercion nor try to coerce them; be open to persuasion and try to persuade them.
> 6. Acceptance. Even if they reject us and our concerns as unworthy of their consideration, accept them as worthy of our consideration, care about them, and be open to learning from them. (p. 38; bold type omitted)

Few, if any, of us follow the six guidelines in our "normal," everyday communication with others. In order to apply Fisher and Brown's guidelines, we must be mindful. As Brodie (1989) points out, "what is unconscious is not within a person's control, but what is made conscious is available for human beings to understand, to change, or to reinforce" (p. 16).

ASSESSING HOW YOU MANAGE CONFLICT WITH STRANGERS

The questionnaire in Table 7.1 is designed to help you assess how you manage conflict with strangers. Take a few minutes to complete it now.

Scores on the questionnaire range from 5 to 25. The higher your score, the greater your potential for successfully managing conflict with strangers. If your score is on the "low" side, remember that managing conflict successfully requires that we be mindful of the *process* of our communication.

❑ Developing Relationships

Most of our close interpersonal relationships are with people who are relatively similar to us. Part of the reason for this is that we do not have a lot of contact with strangers. Another reason why we do not have many close relationships with strangers is that our initial interactions and superficial contacts with strangers often result in ineffective communication. Because our communication with strangers is not as effective and satisfying as we would like, we do not *try* to develop intimate relationships with strangers. If we understand the process of relationship development, however, we can make an informed conscious decision as to whether or not we want to have intimate relationships with strangers. In making such a decision, it is important to keep in mind that the more we know about strangers, the more accurately we can predict their behavior (Honeycutt, Knapp, & Powers, 1983).

COMMUNICATION SATISFACTION

One aspect of developing relationships with strangers is the degree to which we are satisfied with strangers' communication with us and strangers are satisfied with our communication with them. Satisfaction is an affective (i.e., emotional) reaction to communication that meets or fails to meet our

Table 7.1 Assessing Your Management of Conflict with Strangers

The purpose of this questionnaire is to help you assess your ability to success-fully manage conflict with strangers. Respond to each statement by indicating the degree to which it is true regarding how you manage conflict with strang-ers: "Always False" (answer 1), "Usually False" (answer 2), "Sometimes True and Sometimes False" (answer 3), "Usually True" (answer 4), or "Always True" (answer 5).

_____ 1. I balance emotion with reason when trying to manage conflicts with strangers.

_____ 2. I try to understand the strangers with whom I am having a conflict.

_____ 3. I consult strangers before deciding on matters that affect them.

_____ 4. I act reliably (i.e., consistently) when trying to manage conflict with strangers.

_____ 5. I am open to being persuaded when I have conflict with strangers.

To find your score, add the numbers you wrote next to each statement. Scores range from 5 to 25. The higher your score, the greater your potential to success-fully manage conflict with strangers.

SOURCE: The statements are adapted from Fisher and Brown's (1988) work.

expectations (Hecht, 1978). Tsukasa Nishida, Elizabeth Chua, and I (Gudykunst, Nishida, & Chua, 1986, 1987) examined factors that contribute to communication satisfaction in inter-personal relationships between Japanese and North Americans.

Our research indicates that the more communication in a relationship is personalized and synchronized, and the less difficulty people experience in communicating with their part-ner, the more satisfied they are with the communication in their relationship. We also found that the more partners self-disclose to each other, the more they are attracted to each other, the more similarities they perceive, and the more uncertainty they reduce about each other, the more satisfied they are. Fi-nally, the more "competent" the partners judge each others' communication to be, the more satisfied they are.

Michael Hecht and Sydney Ribeau and their associates exam-ined satisfaction with interethnic conversations in the United

States. Hecht, Ribeau, and Alberts (1989), for example, isolated seven factors that contribute to Afro-Americans' satisfaction with their conversations with whites. The first factor necessary for satisfaction is "acceptance." To be satisfied, Afro-Americans need to feel that they are respected, confirmed, and accepted by the whites with whom they communicate. Satisfying conversations with whites also included "emotional expression" and the whites being "authentic" (i.e., whites in satisfying conversations were perceived as "genuine" and whites in dissatisfying conversations were perceived as "evasive"). Afro-Americans also perceived that there was "understanding" (i.e., shared meanings) and "goal attainment" in satisfying conversations. They perceived "negative stereotyping" and felt "powerless" (e.g., manipulated or controlled) in dissatisfying conversations.

Hecht, Ribeau, and Sedano (1990) conducted a similar study with Mexican-Americans. They also found seven factors associated with satisfying and dissatisfying conversations. Similar to Afro-Americans, Mexican-Americans see "acceptance" as an important aspect of satisfying conversations. Satisfying conversations with whites also included the "expression of feelings" and "behaving rationally." The presence of "self-expression" and "relational solidarity" also contributed to satisfaction in conversations. "Negative stereotyping" and failure to discover a shared "worldview" (i.e., absence of perceived similarities) emerged as important factors in dissatisfying conversations.

Three themes are common to these studies. It, therefore, appears clear that whites need to communicate acceptance, express emotions, and avoid negative stereotyping in order for Afro-Americans and Mexican-Americans to be satisfied with their conversations with them. While it was not specifically examined, we can infer that these three factors must be present for Afro-Americans and Mexican-Americans to perceive their white conversational partners as "competent."

ASSESSING YOUR SATISFACTION IN
COMMUNICATING WITH STRANGERS

The questionnaire in Table 7.2 is designed to help you assess your satisfaction with your communication with strangers. Take a couple of minutes to complete the questionnaire now.

Scores on the questionnaire range from 5 to 25. The higher your score, the greater your satisfaction with communicating with strangers. Even though your perceptions of how you communicate with strangers are different than the strangers' perceptions, you also can "reverse" the statements in Table 7.2 and assess your perceptions of your communication with strangers. Remember, however, that how you think you are coming across to strangers may not be the same as how they perceive your communication with them.

DEVELOPING INTIMATE RELATIONSHIPS

There are differences and similarities in how people communicate in interpersonal relationships across cultures. Tsukasa Nishida and I (Gudykunst & Nishida, 1986b), for example, found that people in Japan (a collectivistic culture which emphasizes group membership) perceive ingroup relationships (i.e., co-worker and university classmate) to be more intimate than people in the United States (an individualistic culture which emphasizes the individual). The differences in perceived intimacy of relationships affect the way people communicate.[3] To illustrate, there is a difference in how people in Japan communicate with members of their ingroups and with members of an outgroup, with communication being the most "personal" with ingroups members. In the United States, in contrast, there is not a large difference in how we communicate with members of our ingroups and outgroups, except when outgroup membership is determined by cultural background or ethnicity (Gudykunst et al., in press; Gudykunst & Hammer, 1988a).

In addition to the cultural differences in perceived intimacy, there are many similarities across cultures. People in Japan and

Table 7.2 Assessing Your Communication Satisfaction with Strangers

The purpose of this questionnaire is to help you assess the satisfaction you have when you communicate with strangers. Respond to each statement by indicating the degree to which it is true of your communication with strangers: "Always False" (answer 1), "Usually False" (answer 2), "Sometimes True and Sometimes False" (answer 3), "Usually True" (answer 4), or "Always True" (answer 5).

_____ 1. I am satisfied with my communication with strangers.

_____ 2. I am able to present myself as I want to when I communicate with strangers.

_____ 3. I enjoy communicating with strangers.

_____ 4. Conversations flow smoothly when I communicate with strangers.

_____ 5. I get to say what I want to say when I communicate with strangers.

To find your score, add the numbers you wrote next to each statement. Scores range from 5 to 25. The higher your score, the greater your satisfaction in communicating with strangers.

SOURCE: Adapted from Hecht (1978).

the United States, for example, rate relationships with people they have never met as less intimate than relationships with acquaintances, relationships with acquaintances as less intimate than relationships with friends, and relationships with friends as less intimate than relationships with close friends (Gudykunst & Nishida, 1986b). The similarities in the perceived intimacy of relationships is manifested in our communication. Communication in both cultures becomes more "personal" as the perceived intimacy of the relationship increases (Gudykunst & Nishida, 1986a, 1986b). To illustrate, we talk about more intimate things about ourselves with friends than acquaintances.

Given these similarities and differences across cultures, what happens when people from different cultures communicate? Research suggests that as relationships between people from different cultures become more intimate (i.e., move from initial interactions to close friend), communication becomes more personal; for example, there are increases in self-disclosure, interpersonal attraction, perceived similarities, and uncertainty reduction (Gudykunst, Nishida, & Chua, 1986, 1987). Cultural dissimilarities appear to have a major influence on our communication in the early stages of relationship development (i.e., initial interactions and acquaintance relationships), but not in the final stages (e.g., close friend; Gudykunst, Chua, & Gray, 1987).[4]

I do not want to imply here that cultural and ethnic differences are not "problems" in close relationships. Cultural and ethnic differences can be sources of misunderstandings in intimate relationships, particularly in marital relationships. How to raise children, for example, is a central issue in intercultural or interethnic marriages. Cultural and ethnic differences can be major problems if the partners are not mindful of their communication around core issues like this. While there may be problems in close relationships due to cultural or ethnic differences, cultural and ethnic differences have less of an effect on communication in close friendships than in acquaintance relationships.[5] The nature of the relationship development process itself appears to offer a reasonable explanation as to why cultural and ethnic dissimilarities do not influence communication in close friendships as much as earlier stages of relationships.[6]

In early stages of relationship development, we must rely on cultural and sociological data to predict another person's behavior because we do not have sufficient information to use psychological data in making predictions. As the relationship develops and we gather information about the other person, we begin to use psychological data. When we use psychological data, we are differentiating how the other person is similar to and different from other members of his or her groups. In other words, we no longer rely on our stereotypes to predict the other person's behavior.

What is it about our initial interactions and our communication with acquaintances who are from other groups that allows the relationship to develop into a "friendship"? Research suggests that we must communicate in a way that signals we accept the other person, we must express our feelings, and we must avoid negative stereotyping. All of these factors combined suggested that our communication with the other person helps him or her have positive personal and social identities. Stated differently, we support the other person's self-concept.[7]

Research several colleagues and I conducted (Sudweeks, Gudykunst, Ting-Toomey, & Nishida, 1990; Gudykunst, Gao, Sudweeks, Ting-Toomey, & Nishida, 1991) further suggests that we must perceive some degree of similarity between ourselves and the other person if an intimate relationship is to develop.[8] The display of empathy and mutual accommodation regarding differences in communi-

> *Communicating on automatic pilot filters out strangers as potential friends— communication with them is less effective.*

cation styles (i.e., adapting each other's style to the other person) also appear to be critical.[9] It is also important that at least one person have some competency in the other's language or dialect and that both parties demonstrate some interest in the other's culture or ethnic group.

Other factors that appear to be important are similar to those in developing relationships with people from our own groups. We must, for example, make time available to interact with the other person and consciously or unconsciously attempt to increase the intimacy of our communication (i.e., talk about things that are important to us).[10]

When we communicate on automatic pilot, we filter out strangers as potential friends simply because they are different and our communication with them is not as effective as our communication with people from our own group. Whether or not we want to act differently depends on our motivation. Do we want to approach people who are different, or continue to avoid them? I believe that relationships with strangers provide a chance for us to grow as individuals. The choice about developing these relationships, however, is yours.

I encourage you to make a conscious choice about whether or not you want to communicate effectively and develop

relationships with strangers rather than relying on your unconscious, mindless decisions. If you choose to approach strangers
and are mindful of your communication, you will eventually
discover similarities between yourselves and the strangers with
whom you communicate. The similarities you discover provide
the foundation for developing intimate relationships.

ASSESSING YOUR COMMUNICATION WITH STRANGERS

Table 7.3 contains a questionnaire designed to help you assess
your communication with strangers. Take a few minutes to
complete it now.

Scores on the questionnaire range from 5 to 25. The higher
your score, the greater your potential to develop intimate relationships with strangers.

❑ Building Community

Mother Teresa sees "spiritual deprivation" (i.e., a feeling of
emptiness associated with separation from our fellow humans)
as the major problem facing the world today (Jampolsky, 1989).
One way to deal with this spiritual deprivation is to try to build
community in our lives.

The term community is derived from the Latin *communitas*
which has two related, but distinct interpretations: (1) the quality of "common interest and hence the quality of fellowship,"
and (2) "a body of people having in common an external bond"
(Rosenthal, 1984, p. 219). Yankelovich (1981) argues that community evokes the "feeling that 'Here is where I belong, these
are my people, I care for them, they care for me, I am part of
them' . . . its absence is experienced as an achy loss, a void . . .
feelings of isolation, falseness, instability, and impoverishment
of spirit" (p. 227).

Table 7.3 Assessing Your Communication with Strangers

The purpose of this questionnaire is to help you assess how you communicate with strangers. Respond to each statement by indicating the degree to which it is true of your communication with strangers: "Always False" (answer 1), "Usually False" (answer 2), "Sometimes True and Sometimes False" (answer 3), "Usually True" (answer 4), or "Always True" (answer 5).

_____ 1. I accept strangers as they are.

_____ 2. I express my feelings when I communicate with strangers.

_____ 3. I avoid negative stereotyping when I communicate with strangers.

_____ 4. I find similarities between myself and strangers when we communicate.

_____ 5. I accommodate my behavior to strangers when we communicate.

To find your score, add the numbers you wrote next to each statement. Scores range from 5 to 25. The higher your score, the greater your potential for developing intimate relationships with strangers.

THE NATURE OF COMMUNITY

Martin Buber (1958, 1965) sees community as a choice around a common center; the voluntary coming together of people in a direct relationship that involves a concern for the self, other, and group. He believes that community must begin in small groups and that it cannot be forced on organizations or nations. At the same time, Buber contends that some form of community is necessary to make life worth living.

In Buber's view, a community is *not* a group of likeminded people; rather, it is a group of individuals with complementary natures who have differing minds. Extending Buber's analysis, Maurice Friedman (1983) draws a distinction between a "community of otherness" and a "community of affinity." A community of affinity is a group of likeminded people who have come together for security. Friedman argues that they feel safe because they use a similar language and the same slogans, but they do not have close relations with one another. A community of otherness, on the other hand, begins from the assumption that each member has a different point of view that contributes to the group. Members are not alike, but they share common concerns.

Buber sees openness, *not* intimacy, as one of the keys to developing community. "A real community need not consist of people who are perpetually together; but it must consist of people who, precisely because they are comrades, have mutual access to one another and are ready for one another" (quoted by Friedman, 1986, p. xiii). The importance of openness becomes clear when we look at the distinctions Buber draws among three forms of communication: monologue, technical dialogue, and dialogue. Monologues are "self-centered" conversations in which the other person is treated as an object. Technical dialogues are information centered conversations. Monologues and technical dialogues are necessary and appropriate at times, but problems emerge when they are used too frequently; that is, there is a lack of connection between the participants and community, therefore, cannot develop. For community to develop, dialogue is necessary. Dialogue involves communication between individuals. In a dialogue, each participant's feeling of control and ownership is minimized; each participant confirms the other, even when conflict occurs.

Developing community for Buber requires a commitment to values higher than our own (Arnett, 1986). In his book *Community: Reflections on a Tragic Ideal*, Glenn Tinder (1980) suggests that the values of civility, and tolerance of plurality and diversity are necessary for community. It is important to recognize that holding these values requires that we accept that our own needs are not always met (Arnett, 1986).

The key to building community in Buber's view is for individuals to walk a "narrow ridge." The concept of narrow ridge involves taking both our own and others' viewpoints into consideration in our dealings with others. Robert Arnett (1986) uses the metaphor of a tightrope walker to illustrate the narrow ridge concept. If a tightrope walker leans too much in one direction he or she will begin to loose his or her balance. To regain her or his balance, the tightrope walker must compensate by leaning in the other direction. The same is true of walking the narrow ridge in our dealings with others. If we give our own opinions too much weight in a conversation, we must compensate by giving the others' opinions equal weight if we are going to walk a narrow ridge.

In walking the narrow ridge, we must try to understand the others' point of view. Buber does not advocate that we take a nonjudgmental or relativistic attitude toward others. Rather, he argues that we openly listen to others, but if we are not persuaded by their arguments, we should maintain our original position; if we are persuaded, we should modify our opinions. There is a subtle difference between listening openly and not changing our minds, or being closed-minded. The difference depends on our intentions. If our intentions are to consider others' opinions seriously, we are walking the narrow ridge; if our intentions are not to consider others' opinions, then we are closed-minded. It is the dual concern for self and other in walking the narrow ridge that stops polarized communication and allows community to develop (Arnett, 1986).

Walking the narrow ridge with strangers does not require that we stop categorizing others. Categorization cannot occur without its complementary process, particularization—differentiating others from their groups (Billig, 1987). Walking the narrow ridge requires particularization, but it does not require the elimination of categorization.

Buber argues that we should avoid giving in and accepting others' opinions just for the sake of "peace." Rather, he suggests that we should accept others' opinions or compromise if it is the way to the "best" solution. Our commitment must be to principles, not false peace. It is also important to note that Buber does not suggest that we accept everything others say unquestioningly. Suspicion is sometimes warranted, but problems occur when suspicion becomes a norm of communication. When suspicion is always present, however, existential mistrust exists.

One factor that contributes to mistrust in low-context, individualistic cultures like the United States' that value direct communication is looking for hidden meanings. Suspicion and looking for hidden meanings are only two of the factors that lead to mistrust. No matter how mistrust comes about, it always polarizes communication. Understanding strangers requires "a willing suspension of disbelief" (Trilling, 1968, p. 106).

> *It is community that makes life worth living.*

PRINCIPLES OF COMMUNITY BUILDING

To summarize, a community consists of diverse individuals who are honest and open with each other, trust each other, engage in ethical behavior, and are committed to living together. Members of a community are civil to each other, and they value diversity while, at the same time, they search for the commonalities humans share. Community is desirable because, as Buber points out, it is community that makes life worth living. Further, it is the existence of community that will make peace and intergroup harmony possible. While community occurs in groups, individuals must take the responsibility for building community in their marriages, workplaces, schools, cities, nations, and the world.

To conclude, I want to synthesize the information presented into a set of "principles" for community building. The principles presented are based on several *assumptions* which I take for granted:

(1) Community is necessary to make life worth living and increase the potential for peace in the world.

(2) Developing community is the responsibility of the individual. Each of us must take the responsibility for building community in our own lives.

(3) Cultural and ethnic diversity (and all other forms of diversity, as well) are necessary resources for building community. A true community cannot exist without diversity.

(4) Communities can be any size (e.g., a marriage, social organization, university, town, country, or even the world), but we must start building community in the smaller groups of which we are members (e.g., families) and work toward developing community in the larger groups (e.g., universities).

(5) We are what we think. Gerald Jampolsky (1989), among others, points out that "everything in life depends on the thoughts we choose to hold in our minds and our willingness to change our belief systems" (p. 31). Similarly, in *The Dhammapada*, Buddha said that "our life is shaped by our minds; we become what we think."

(6) Community cannot exist without conflict. Stuart Hampshire (1989) argues that we should expect "ineliminable and acceptable conflicts, and . . . rationally controlled hostilities, as the normal condition" (p. 189). To develop community, individuals must engage in "graceful fighting"; try to persuade each other, but not coerce each other (Peck, 1987). Be committed to principles, not being right (Buber, 1965).

(7) As Fisher and Brown suggest, one person can change a relationship and/or start the development of community. If one person follows the principles suggested below, people with whom this person comes in contact will change their behavior.

Given these assumptions and the material summarized in this chapter, I have derived seven community building principles:

(1) *Be Committed.* We must be committed to the principle of building community in our lives, as well as to the individuals with whom we are trying to develop a community (Peck, 1987). Commitment to others is prerequisite for community to exist.

(2) *Be Mindful.* Think about what we do and say. Focus on the process, not the outcome (Langer, 1989). Be contemplative in examining our own behavior (Nozick, 1989) and that of the communities of which we are members (Peck, 1987).

(3) *Be Unconditionally Accepting.* Accept others as they are; do not try to change or control them (Fisher & Brown, 1988). Value diversity and do not judge others based only on their diversity. Minimize expectations, prejudices, suspicion, and mistrust (Peck, 1987).

(4) *Be Concerned for Both Yourself and Others.* We must walk a narrow ridge in our interactions with others whenever practical; avoid polarized communication (Arnett, 1986) and engage in dialogue whenever possible (Buber, 1958, 1965). Consult others on issues that affect them and be open to their ideas (Fisher & Brown, 1988). Fight gracefully (Peck, 1987).

(5) *Be Understanding.* Strive to understand others as completely as possible. As Martin Luther King, Jr. (1963) said, "shallow understanding from people of good will is more frustrating than absolute misunderstanding from people of ill will" (p. 88). Determine how others' interpretations of events and/or behaviors are different from and similar to our own. Recognize how culture, ethnicity, and so forth affect the way we think and behave. Search for commonalities on which community can be built. Balance emotion, anxiety, and fear with reason (Fisher & Brown, 1988).

(6) *Be Ethical.* Engage in behavior that is not a means to an end, but behavior that is morally right in and of itself (Bellah et al., 1985). Be reliable in what we say and do (Fisher & Brown, 1988). Be morally inclusive (Optow, 1990); engage in service to others (Lynberg, 1989).

(7) *Be Peaceful.* Do not be violent, deceitful, breach valid promises, or be secretive (Bok, 1989). Even if others engage in these behaviors toward us we are not justified in engaging in these behaviors toward them (Gandhi, 1948; King, 1958). As Socrates pointed out, retaliation is never justified (Vlastos, in press). Strive for internal harmony (Prather, 1986) and harmony in relations with others.

These seven "principles" are ideals for which we can strive. The more we are able to put them into practice individually, the greater the chance for community and peace in the world. We must not, however, be "hard" on ourselves when we fail to achieve the ideal. Achieving these ideals is a lifetime's work and requires extensive practice. If we are to tolerate others, we must begin by accepting our own "mistakes." As Hugh Prather (1986) points out, when we find that we are not engaging in behaviors we want to practice (e.g., building community), we must "forgive" ourselves and start anew at practicing the behaviors. For most of us, this will occur numerous times a day initially. The behaviors suggested in the ideals are different from those we have learned from birth. To engage in these behaviors consistently, we must "unlearn" many of our "normal" behaviors (e.g., behaviors that occur at low levels of awareness such as reacting "defensively" and looking out only for ourselves). The critical thing is *not* the outcome, but the process. If we *try* to behave in a way consistent with these ideals (the process), community (the desirable outcome) will occur.

Notes

❑ **Chapter 1**

   1. This idea originally was used in *Communicating with Strangers* (Gudykunst & Kim, 1984; Kim & Gudykunst, in press). This book differs from the earlier text I co-authored in several ways. First, because of its length, the present book is less comprehensive in the material covered. I have selected the material the theory suggests is critical to incorporate here. Second, this book is much more "applied" than the earlier text. My focus here is on presenting material that can be used to improve communication effectiveness. I take a "culture general" approach; that is, I present general strategies for reducing uncertainty and anxiety that can be applied when you communicate with people from a variety of cultural and ethnic groups.

   2. Howell suggests a fifth stage, "conscious supercompetence," which is not included here. I have described his stages in the language I use throughout the book.

3. I have modified and extended the theory since this published version was completed. A complete elaboration will appear in Gudykunst (in progress). Where I draw on extensions in this book, I will outline the theoretical rationale in notes.

4. Most of the questionnaires presented are adapted from reliable and valid measures used in research. Some I developed for the purpose of the book. While I have not assessed the psychometric properties of the questionnaires, I believe they are all reasonable measures of the concepts under discussion.

5. Some of the ideas for this introduction were drawn from Fisher (1978).

6. My view of the nature of communication draws upon many different sources (e.g., Barnlund, 1962; Berger & Bradac, 1982; Berlo, 1960; Miller & Steinberg, 1975). It is influenced most by Miller and Steinberg (1975). I disagree with them in one important area, however. They argue that communication is an intentional activity. I will argue that communication can occur unintentionally. Here and throughout the book I will attempt to keep references to a minimum. The general sources for this section are specified above. When I use a specific scholar's position, I will cite the source in the text.

7. See Stewart (1990) for a detailed discussion of the transactional model of communication.

8. As indicated earlier, Miller and Steinberg (1975) take this position.

9. The sources of behavior discussed below are based originally on the work of Harry Triandis (1977, 1980). The specific discussion here is drawn from my extension of his work (Gudykunst, 1987; Gudykunst & Ting-Toomey, 1988).

10. I will draw on models of cognitive therapy throughout the book, especially Beck (1988).

11. These two functions are drawn from my theory of interpersonal and intergroup communication (Gudykunst, 1988). I extended the work of Charles Berger and his associates (e.g., Berger & Bradac, 1982; Berger & Calabrese, 1975) on uncertainty reduction and Stephan and Stephan (1985) on anxiety reduction.

12. A complete list of the factors contributing to the uncertainty and anxiety we experience can be found in the general version of the theory on which the book is based (Gudykunst, 1988) and a special version of the theory designed to explain intercultural adaptation (Gudykunst & Hammer, 1988b).

13. I am basing the argument made here on Byrne and Kelley's (1981) discussion of the relationship between anxiety and test performance.

14. While it is awkward usage, I will talk about people from the United States rather than "Americans." The reason for this is that use of the term Americans to refer to people from the United States often is considered offensive by people from Mexico, and Latin and South America who are also "Americans." Where possible, I will use North Americans, but this term is also problematic.

15. This discussion is drawn from social identity theory (e.g., Tajfel, 1978; Tajfel & Turner, 1979) and ethnolinguistic identity theory (e.g., Giles & Johnson, 1987).

16. Douglas (1986) also points out that we derive social identities from the institutions with which we are associated.

17. See Boulding (1988) for a discussion of "species identity."

❏ **Chapter 2**

1. Rogers and Kincaid actually use the term cognitions instead of attaching meaning. I have used attaching meaning to be consistent with the position I outline below. McLeod and Chaffee (1973) refer to mutual understanding as "accuracy" in their coorientational model.

2. Beck (1988) cites research on marital communication (e.g., Noller, 1980) to support this claim.

3. See Chapter 7 in Beck (1988) for an extended discussion of this process.

4. Billig (1987) argues that categorization is a "thoughtless" process and that the dialectic between categorization and particularization constitutes thinking. While on the surface it appears that his argument is inconsistent with Langer's position, I believe they are compatible.

5. I have never been able to trace where the distinction among description, interpretation, and evaluations originated. The earliest source I have located is Berlo (1960). My introduction to applying the idea to improve communication effectiveness came from Milton and Janet Bennett when I facilitated the Intercultural Communication Workshop at the University of Minnesota. John Wendt wrote a handout on it for workshop facilitators.

6. See, for example, Roach and Wyatt (1988) and Rogers (1980).

7. The reason for this is that active and empathic listening emerged from therapeutic relationships (i.e., they were suggested as techniques counselors should use when communicating with their patients). The therapeutic relationship is, by definition, one-sided.

8. While Stewart and thomas do not refer to his work, their approach clearly is based on the work of Martin Buber. Buber's approach to dialogue is discussed in the last chapter of this book.

❏ **Chapter 3**

1. There are other ways of talking about culture. Joel Garreau (1981), for example, isolates nine nations of North America (e.g., Mexamerica, Dixie, Quebec, The Islands, New England, The Foundry, The Breadbasket, Ecotopia, The Empty Quarter). He argues that each of the nine nations shares a common culture.

2. For a complete discussion of the various dimensions that could be used see Gudykunst and Ting-Toomey (1988).

3. See Hofstede (1980), Kluckkohn and Strodtbeck (1961), and Triandis (1988) for extended discussions of this dimension of cultural variability. It should be noted that this dimension is not only isolated by theorists in "western" cultures, but is also isolated by theorists from "eastern" cultures (see Chinese Culture Connection, 1987, for an example).

4. Greeley (1989) argues that individualism-collectivism differences can be applied to religious denominations; protestants are individualistic and catholics are collectivistic.

5. Triandis, Brislin, and Hui (1988) provide concrete suggestions for individualists interacting with collectivists and collectivists interacting with individualists.

6. I do not mean to say that everyone's ideas of ethnicity have changed. The predominate view, however, has changed from assimilationist to pluralistic.

7. Park actually used the term "race" not ethnic group. I am avoiding the use of the term race throughout the book. There are several reasons for this. The major reason is that the term race is emotionally loaded for many people, while ethnicity is not. Moreover, it is the shared cultural characteristics of a racial group (i.e., their ethnicity) that influences their communication patterns.

8. Edwards (1985) makes the point that language is not necessary for an ethnic group to survive as a unique group.

9. For an excellent discussion of white ethnicity and the use of labels, see Alba (1990).

10. This position is consistent with Gilligan's (1982) work on differences in moral development between men and women.

11. To the best of my knowledge there is no specific research supporting this contention. For a complete elaboration of the logic and suggestions for research, see Skevington (1989).

12. Beck also indicates there are differences in the intimacy of the topics men and women discuss. I have not included this difference because the research findings are mixed.

13. See Tannen (1990) for a more complete discussion of this topic.

14. For a review of this research, see Dahnke (1983).

15. See Rubin (1990) for an excellent discussion of anti-Semitism. Tempest's (1990) article also provides a summary of recent examples of anti-Semitism.

❑ **Chapter 4**

1. Burgoon and Hale do not limit their statement to this group, I do.

2. See Stephan and Stephan (1989) for several citations to support this claim.

3. This statement may only apply to in the presence of "educated" individuals. In Chapter 1, I quoted Spike Lee (1990) as saying "racism is fashionable today." I believe that both statements are "true" in specific contexts.

4. For excellent examples, see the Frontline video "Racism 101" or issues of newsmagazines that focused on this topic in the first six months of 1990.

5. See Vassiliou, Triandis, Vassiliou, and McGuire (1972) for a complete discussion of the complexity of stereotypes.

6. For a recent review of research on categorization and category representations, see Messick and Mackie (1989).

7. See Jussim, Coleman, and Lerch (1987) for a summary of the major theories of stereotyping.

8. See Giles, Mulac, Bradac, and Johnson (1987) for a review of research on accommodation.

❑ Chapter 5

1. Kelley uses an analysis of variance statistical analogy to explain this process.

2. See Pettigrew (1982) for a summary of the findings from over 100 studies of category width.

3. For a complete discussion of the cultural differences in how uncertainty is reduced, see Gudykunst and Ting-Toomey (1988).

❑ Chapter 6

1. Spitzberg and Cupach (1984) use the term effectiveness to refer to task outcomes (e.g., goal achievement).

2. Watzlawick, Beavin, and Jackson (1967), for example, point out that the way members of a family communicate with each other can create mental illness.

3. J. H. Turner (1987) uses different labels for some of the terms (including the needs). He uses the term ethnomethods, for example, to refer to what I call habits or scripts. I believe my terms capture the essence of his idea, but are not as full of academic jargon.

4. Spitzberg and Cupach (1984) also talk about approach avoidance as a factor in motivation. They, however, assume that it is a basic orientation to any encounter rather than deriving it from more basic needs as I am here.

5. Langer notes that there appear to be "taboo" questions. I believe, however, that most of the taboos are in our minds.

6. Berger (1979) actually isolates a third interactive strategy, deception detection, that I am not discussing.

7. See Gouldner (1960) for an extensive discussion.

8. There are some differences in how it is manifested in different cultures. See Gudykunst and Ting-Toomey (1988) for a detailed discussion.

9. The theory (Gudykunst, 1988) suggests that effectiveness and adaptation are functions of reducing uncertainty and anxiety. Other variables (e.g., expectations) affect our level of uncertainty and anxiety and are not linked directly to effectiveness. Gao and Gudykunst (1990) tested this assumption in an adaptation context and it was supported. There are numerous other skills that could be discussed if I did not select the skills based on the theory. There is some

overlap between those selected on the basis of the theory and atheoretically derived lists of skills. Ruben (1976), for example, listed seven skills: (1) empathy, (2) tolerance for ambiguity, (3) display of respect, (4) interaction posture, (5) orientation to knowledge, (6) role behavior, and (7) interaction management.

10. Space does not permit an elaborate discussion of ethical issues here. A complete discussion of ethical relativity theory can be found in *Communicating with Strangers* (first edition: Gudykunst & Kim, 1984; second edition: Kim & Gudykunst, in press).

11. The way I am talking about behavioral flexibility is very similar to Lennox and Wolfe's (1984) notion of ability to modify self-presentations (which is a subscale in their revised self-monitoring scale). Spitzberg and Cupach (1984) included Snyder's (1974) notion of self-monitoring as a skill in communication competence. I have not called this self-monitoring or ability to modify self-presentations because I think the idea of behavioral flexibility is more general. The concepts, however, are interrelated.

❑ Chapter 7

1. I have cited only representative studies here. For a more detailed discussion, see Gudykunst and Ting-Toomey (1988).

2. My focus below is on black-white differences. Japanese-American, Chinese-American, and Mexican-American patterns are similar to the cultural differences cited above. For other examples, see Boucher, Landis, and Clark (1987), and Strobe, Kruglanski, Bar-Tal, and Hewstone (1988).

3. This research was an extension of Knapp, Ellis, and Williams' (1980) research in the United States.

4. There are differences in the relationship labels used in the various studies. I have used the labels isolated above for illustrative purposes.

5. There obviously will be exceptions here. A man may want an "Oriental" wife, for example, because he thinks she will be passive and serve him.

6. Much of the argument I make in this section is drawn from Gudykunst (1989).

7. Self-concept support has been found to be critical in relationship development. See Cushman and Cahn (1985) for a summary of this research. These factors also are related to Bell and Daly's (1984) "concern and caring" affinity-seeking strategy.

8. See Gudykunst (1989) for a summary of this research. Similarity is part of Bell and Daly's (1984) "commonalities" affinity-seeking strategy.

9. This is related to Bell and Daly's (1984) "politeness" affinity-seeking strategy.

10. These issues are related to Bell and Daly's "other involvement" affinity-seeking strategy.

References

Abelson, R. (1976). Script processing in attitude formation and decision making. In J. Carroll & J. Payne (Eds.), *Cognition and social behavior*. Hillsdale, NJ: Lawrence Erlbaum.

Adler, N. (1986). *International dimensions of organizational behavior*. Boston: Kent.

Alba, R. (1990). *Ethnic identity: The transformation of white America*. New Haven, CT: Yale University Press.

Allport, G. (1954). *The nature of prejudice*. New York: Macmillan.

Arnett, R. C. (1986). *Communication and community*. Carbondale: Southern Illinois University Press.

Ashford, S., & Cummings, L. (1983). Feedback as an individual resource. *Organizational Behavior and Human Performance, 32*, 370-398.

Ball-Rokeach, S. (1973). From pervasive ambiguity to definition of the situation. *Sociometry, 36*, 378-389.

Barnlund, D. (1962). Toward a meaning centered philosophy of communication. *Journal of Communication, 2*, 197-211.

Barnlund, D. (1975). *Public and private self in Japan and the United States*. Tokyo: Simul.

Barth, F. (1969). *Ethnic groups and boundaries*. London: Allen & Unwin.

Beck, A. (1988). *Love is never enough*. New York: Harper & Row.

Bell, R., & Daly, J. (1984). The affinity-seeking function of communication. *Communication Monographs, 51*, 91-115.

Bellah, R. N., Madsen, R., Sullivan, W. M., Swidler, A., & Tipton, S. M. (1985). *Habits of the heart: Individualism and commitment in American life*. Berkeley: University of California Press.

Bennett, M. (1979). Overcoming the Golden Rule: Sympathy and empathy. In D. Nimmo (Ed.), *Communication yearbook 3*. New Brunswick, NJ: Transaction Books.

Berger, C. R. (1979). Beyond initial interactions. In H. Giles & R. St. Clair (Eds.), *Language and social psychology*. Oxford, UK: Basil Blackwell.

Berger, C. R., & Bradac, J. (1982). *Language and social knowledge*. London: Edward Arnold.

Berger, C. R., & Calabrese, R. (1975). Some explorations in initial interactions and beyond: Toward a developmental theory of interpersonal communication. *Human Communication Research, 1*, 99-112.

Berger, C. R., & Douglas, W. (1982). Thought and talk. In F. Dance (Ed.), *Human communication theory*. New York: Harper & Row.

Berger, C. R., Gardner, R., Parks, M., Shulman, L., & Miller, G. (1976). Interpersonal epistemology and interpersonal communication. In G. Miller (Ed.), *Explorations in interpersonal communication*. Beverly Hills, CA: Sage.

Berlo, D. (1960). *The process of communication*. New York: Holt.

Billig, M. (1987). *Arguing and thinking*. Cambridge, UK: Cambridge University Press.

Bok, S. (1989). *A strategy for peace: Human values and the threat of war*. New York: Pantheon.

Bond, M. H., Wan, K., Leung, K., & Giacalone, R. (1985). How are the responses to verbal insults related to cultural collectivism and power distance? *Journal of Cross-Cultural Psychology, 16*, 111-127.

Boucher, K., Landis, D., & Clark, K. (Eds.). (1987). *Ethnic conflict*. Newbury Park, CA: Sage.

Boulding, E. (1988). *Building a global civic culture*. Syracuse, NY: Syracuse University Press.

Boyer, E. (1990, June 20). Letter to the editor. *Chronicle of Higher Education*, p. B4.

Breakwell, G. (1979). Women: Group and identity. *Women's Studies International Quarterly, 2*, 9-17.

Brewer, M. B. (1981). Ethnocentrism and its role in interpersonal trust. In M. Brewer & B. Collins (Eds.), *Scientific inquiry and the social sciences*. San Francisco: Jossey-Bass.

Brewer, M. B., & Miller, N. (1988). Contact and cooperation: When do they work? In P. Katz & D. Taylor (Eds.), *Eliminating racism*. New York: Plenum.

Brislin, R. W., Cushner, K., Cherrie, C., & Yong, M. (1986). *Intercultural interactions: A practical guide*. Beverly Hills, CA: Sage.

Brodie, H. K. (1989, September 9). No we're not taught to hate, but we can overcome instinct to fear 'the other.' *Los Angeles Times*, Part II, p. 16.

Buber, M. (1958). *I and thou*. New York: Scribner.

Buber, M. (1965). *Between man and man*. New York: Macmillan.

Burgoon, J., & Hale, J. (1988). Nonverbal expectancy violations. *Communication Monographs, 55*, 58-79.

Byrne, D., & Kelley, K. (1981). *An introduction to personality* (3rd ed.). Englewood Cliffs, NJ: Prentice-Hall.

Carroll, R. (1988). *Cultural misunderstandings: The French-American experience.* Chicago: University of Chicago Press.

Chinese Culture Connection. (1987). Chinese values and the search for culture-free dimensions of culture. *Journal of Cross-Cultural Psychology, 18,* 143-164.

Condor, S. (1986). Sex role beliefs and "traditional" women. In S. Wilkenson (Ed.), *Feminist social psychology.* Milton Keynes, UK: Open University Press.

Copeland, L. (1988). Valuing workplace diversity. *Personnel Administrator, 11,* 38-39.

Crockett, W., & Friedman, P. (1980). Theoretical explorations in the process of initial interactions. *Western Journal of Speech Communication, 44,* 86-92.

Csikszentmihalyi, M. (1990). *Flow: The psychology of optimal experience.* New York: Harper & Row.

Cushman, D. P., & Cahn, D. (1985). *Interpersonal communication.* Albany: State University of New York Press.

Dahnke, G. (1983). Communication between handicapped and nonhandicapped. In M. McLaughlin (Ed.), *Communication yearbook 6.* Beverly Hills, CA: Sage.

Davidson, A., & Thompson, E. (1980). Cross-cultural studies of attitudes and beliefs. In H. Triandis & R. Brislin (Eds.), *Handbook of cross-cultural psychology* (Vol. 5). Boston: Allyn & Bacon.

Detweiler, R. (1975). On inferring the intentions of a person from another culture. *Journal of Personality, 43,* 591-611.

Detweiler, R. (1978). Culture, category width, and attributions. *Journal of Cross-Cultural Psychology, 11,* 101-124.

Deutsch, K. (1968). Toward a cybernetic model of man and society. In W. Buckley (Ed.), *Modern systems theory for the behavioral scientist.* Chicago: Aldine.

Devine, P. (1989). Stereotypes and prejudice. *Journal of Personality and Social Psychology, 56,* 5-18.

DeVos, G. (1975). Ethnic pluralism. In G. DeVos & L. Romanucci-Ross (Eds.), *Ethnic identity.* Palo Alto, CA: Mayfield.

Douglas, M. (1986). *How institutions think.* Syracuse, NY: Syracuse University Press.

Duncan, B. (1976). Differential social perception and attribution of intergroup violence. *Journal of Personality and Social Psychology, 34,* 590-598.

Edwards, J. (1975). *Language, society, and identity.* Oxford, UK: Basil Blackwell.

Ehrenhaus, P. (1983). Culture and the attribution process. In W. Gudykunst (Ed.), *Intercultural communication theory.* Beverly Hills, CA: Sage.

Erickson, F. (1981). *Anecdote, rhapsody, and rhetoric.* Paper presented at the Georgetown University Roundtable on Language and Linguistics, Washington, DC.

Fisher, B. A. (1978). *Perspectives on human communication.* New York: Macmillan.

Fisher, R., & Brown, S. (1988). *Getting together: Building relationships as we negotiate.* Boston: Houghton Mifflin.

Friedman, M. (1974). *The hidden human image.* New York: Dell.

Friedman, M. (1983). *The confirmation of otherness: In family, community and society.* New York: Pilgrim Press.

Friedman, M. (1986). Foreword. In R. Arnett, *Communication and community.* Carbondale: Southern Illinois University Press.

Gandhi, M. K. (1948). *Nonviolence in peace and war.* Ahmedabad, India: Garland.

Gao, G., & Gudykunst, W. B. (1990). Uncertainty, anxiety, and adaptation. *International Journal of Intercultural Relations, 14,* 301-317.

Garreau, J. (1981). *The nine nations of North America.* Boston: Houghton Mifflin.

Gass, S., & Varonis, E. (1984). The effect of familiarity on the comprehensibility of nonnative speech. *Language Learning, 34,* 65-89.

Gass, S., & Varonis, E. (1985). Variations in native speaker speech modification on nonnative speakers. *Studies in Second Language Acquisition, 7,* 37-58.

Geertz, C. (1966). *Person, time and conduct in Bali.* New Haven, CT: Yale Southeast Asia Studies Program.

Geertz, C. (1973). *The interpretation of cultures.* New York: Basic Books.

Gerbner, G. (1978). The dynamics of cultural resistance. In G. Tuchman et al. (Eds.), *Health and home.* New York: Oxford University Press.

Gibb, J. (1961). Defensive communication. *Journal of Communication, 11,* 141-148.

Giles, H., Bourhis, R., & Taylor, D. (1977). Towards a theory of language in ethnic group relations. In H. Giles (Ed.), *Language, ethnicity, and intergroup relations.* London: Academic Press.

Giles, H., & Johnson, P. (1981). The role of language in ethnic group relations. In J. Turner & H. Giles (Eds.), *Intergroup behavior.* Chicago: University of Chicago Press.

Giles, H., & Johnson, P. (1987). Ethnolinguistic identity theory. *International Journal of the Sociology of Language, 68,* 69-90.

Giles, H., Mulac, A., Bradac, J., & Johnson, P. (1987). Speech accommodation theory. In M. McLaughlin (Ed.), *Communication yearbook 10.* Newbury Park, CA: Sage.

Gilligan, C. (1982). *In a different voice.* Cambridge, MA: Harvard University Press.

Glazer, N., & Moynihan, D. (1975). *Ethnicity.* Cambridge, MA: Harvard University Press.

Gorden, M. (1964). *Assimilation in American life.* Oxford, UK: Oxford University Press.

Gouldner, A. (1960). The norm of reciprocity. *American Sociological Review, 25,* 161-179.

Greeley, A. (1989). Protestant and catholic: Is the analogical imagination extinct? *American Sociological Review, 54,* 485-502.

Gudykunst, W. B. (1987). Cross-cultural comparisons. In C. Berger & S. Chaffee (Eds.), *Handbook of communication science.* Newbury Park, CA: Sage.

Gudykunst, W. B. (1988). Uncertainty and anxiety. In Y. Kim & W. Gudykunst (Eds.), *Theories in intercultural communication.* Newbury Park, CA: Sage.

Gudykunst, W. B. (1989). Culture and communication in interpersonal relationships. In J. Anderson (Ed.), *Communication yearbook 12.* Newbury Park, CA: Sage.

Gudykunst, W. B. (in progress). *Strangeness and familiarity: A theory of interpersonal and intergroup communication.* Newbury Park, CA: Sage.

Gudykunst, W. B., Chua, E., & Gray, A. (1987). Cultural dissimilarities and uncertainty reduction processes. In M. McLaughlin (Ed.), *Communication yearbook 10.* Newbury Park, CA: Sage.

Gudykunst, W. B., Gao, G., Schmidt, K., Nishida, T., Bond, M., Leung, K., Wang, G., & Barraclough, R. (in press). The influence of individualism-collectivism on communication in ingroup and outgroup relationships. *Journal of Cross-Cultural Psychology.*

Gudykunst, W. B., Gao, G., Sudweeks, S., Ting-Toomey, S., & Nishida, T. (1991). Themes in opposite-sex Japanese-North American relationships. In S. Ting-Toomey & F. Korzenny (Eds.), *Cross-cultural interpersonal communication.* Newbury Park, CA: Sage.

Gudykunst, W. B., & Hammer, M. R. (1988a). The influence of social identity and intimacy of interethnic relationships on uncertainty reduction processes. *Human Communication Research, 14,* 569-601.

Gudykunst, W. B., & Hammer, M. R. (1988b). Strangers and hosts. In Y. Kim & W. Gudykunst (Eds.), *Cross-cultural adaptation.* Newbury Park, CA: Sage.

Gudykunst, W. B., & Kim, Y. Y. (1984). *Communicating with strangers: An approach to intercultural communication.* New York: McGraw-Hill.

Gudykunst, W. B., & Nishida, T. (1986a). Attributional confidence in low- and high-context cultures. *Human Communication Research, 12,* 525-549.

Gudykunst, W. B., & Nishida, T. (1986b). The influence of cultural variability on perceptions of communication behavior associated with relationship terms. *Human Communication Research, 13,* 147-166.

Gudykunst, W. B., Nishida, T., & Chua, E. (1986). Uncertainty reduction processes in Japanese-North American relationships. *Communication Research Reports, 3,* 39-46.

Gudykunst, W. B., Nishida, T., & Chua, E. (1987). Perceptions of social penetration in Japanese-North American relationships. *International Journal of Intercultural Relations, 11,* 171-190.

Gudykunst, W. B., & Ting-Toomey, S., with Chua, E. (1988). *Culture and interpersonal communication.* Newbury Park, CA: Sage.

Gumperz, J. (1982). *Discourse strategies.* Cambridge, UK: Cambridge University Press.

Gurin, P., & Townsend, A. (1986). Properties of gender identity and their implications for gender consciousness. *British Journal of Social Psychology, 25,* 139-148.

Hall, E. T. (1959). *The silent language.* Garden City, NY: Doubleday.

Hall, E. T. (1976). *Beyond culture.* Garden City, NY: Doubleday.

Hampshire, S. (1989). *Innocence and experience.* Cambridge, MA: Harvard University Press.

Haslett, B., & Ogilvie, J. (1988). Feedback processes in small groups. In R. Cathcart & L. Samovar (Eds.), *Small group communication: A reader* (5th ed.). Dubuque, IA: William C. Brown.

Hecht, M. (1978). The conceptualization and measurement of communication satisfaction. *Human Communication Research, 4,* 253-264.

Hecht, M., & Ribeau, S. (in press). Sociocultural roots of ethnic identity. *Journal of Black Studies.*

Hecht, M., Ribeau, S., & Alberts, J. (1989). An Afro-American perspective on interethnic communication. *Communication Monographs, 56,* 385-410.

Hecht, M., Ribeau, S., & Sedano, M. (1990). A Mexican-American perspective on interethnic communication. *International Journal of Intercultural Relations, 14,* 31-55.

Heider, F. (1958). *The psychology of interpersonal relations*. New York: John Wiley.

Herman, S., & Schield, E. (1961). The stranger group in a cross-cultural situation. *Sociometry, 24,* 165-176.

Herskovits, M. (1955). *Cultural anthropology*. New York: Knopf.

Hewstone, M., & Brown, R. (1986). Contact is not enough. In M. Hewstone & R. Brown (Eds.), *Contact and conflict in intergroup encounters*. Oxford, UK: Basil Blackwell.

Hewstone, M., & Giles, H. (1986). Stereotypes and intergroup communication. In W. Gudykunst (Ed.), *Intergroup communication*. London: Edward Arnold.

Hewstone, M., & Jaspars, J. (1984). Social dimensions of attributions. In H. Tajfel (Ed.), *The social dimension* (Vol. 2). Cambridge, UK: Cambridge University Press.

Hofman, T. (1985). Arabs and Jews, Blacks and Whites: Identity and group relations. *Journal of Multilingual and Multicultural Development, 6,* 217-237.

Hofstede, G. (1980). *Culture's consequences*. Beverly Hills, CA: Sage.

Hofstede, G., & Bond, M. (1984). Hofstede's culture dimensions. *Journal of Cross-Cultural Psychology, 15,* 417-433.

Honeycutt, J. M., Knapp, M. L., & Powers, W. G. (1983). On knowing others and predicting what they say. *Western Journal of Speech Communication, 47,* 157-174.

Howell, W. S. (1982). *The empathic communicator*. Belmont, CA: Wadsworth.

Hoyle, R., Pinkley, R., & Insko, C. (1989). Perceptions of social behavior: Evidence of differing expectations for interpersonal and intergroup behavior. *Personality and Social Psychology Bulletin, 15,* 365-376.

Hraba, J., & Hoiberg, E. (1983). Origins of modern theories of ethnicity. *Sociological Quarterly, 24,* 381-391.

Hudson Institute. (1987). *Workforce 2000*. Washington, DC: United States Department of Labor.

Jackson, J. (1964). The normative regulation of authoritative behavior. In W. Grove & J. Dyson (Eds.), *The making of decisions*. New York: Free Press.

Jampolsky, G. (1989). *Out of darkness into the light*. New York: Bantam.

Janis, I., & Mann, L. (1977). *Decision making*. New York: Free Press.

Jussim, L., Coleman, L., & Lerch, L. (1987). The nature of stereotypes. *Journal of Personality and Social Psychology, 52,* 536-546.

Kashima, Y., & Triandis, H. C. (1986). The self-serving bias in attributions as a coping strategy. *Journal of Cross-Cultural Psychology, 17,* 83-97.

Katriel, T. (1986). *Talking straight*. Cambridge,UK: Cambridge University Press.

Katz, D., & Braly, K. (1933). Racial stereotypes of 100 college students. *Journal of Abnormal and Social Psychology, 28,* 280-290.

Keesing, R. (1974). Theories of culture. *Annual Review of Anthropology, 3,* 73-97.

Kelley, H. H. (1967). Attribution theory in social psychology. *Nebraska Symposium on Motivation, 15,* 192-238.

Kelley, H. H. (1972). Causal schemata and the attribution process. In E. Jones et al. (Eds.), *Attribution: Perceiving the causes of behavior*. Morristown, NJ: General Learning Press.

Kim, Y. Y., & Gudykunst, W. B. (in press). *Communicating with strangers* (2nd ed.). New York: McGraw-Hill.

King, M. L., Jr. (1958). *Stride toward freedom*. New York: Harper & Row.

King, M. L., Jr. (1963). Letter from Birmingham jail. In *Why we can't wait*. New York: Harper and Row.

Kitayama, S., & Burnstein, E. (1988). Automaticity in conversations. *Journal of Personality and Social Psychology, 54*, 219-224.

Kluckhohn, F., & Strodtbeck, F. (1961). *Variations in value orientations*. New York: Row, Peterson.

Knapp, M., Ellis, D., & Williams, B. (1980). Perceptions of communication behavior associated with relationship terms. *Communication Monographs, 47*, 262-278.

Kochman, T. (1981). *Black and white: Styles in conflict*. Chicago: University of Chicago Press.

Lakoff, R. T. (1990). *Talking power: The politics of language*. New York: Basic Books.

Langer, E. (1978). Rethinking the role of thought in social interaction. In J. Harvey et al. (Eds.), *New directions in attribution research* (Vol. 2). Hillsdale, NJ: Lawrence Erlbaum.

Langer, E. (1989). *Mindfulness*. Reading, MA: Addison-Wesley.

Leary, M., Kowalski, R., & Bergen, D. (1988). Interpersonal information acquisition and confidence in first encounters. *Personality and Social Psychology Bulletin, 14*, 68-77.

Lee, S. (1990, July 12). Interview on *48 Hours*. CBS Television.

Lennox, R., & Wolfe, R. (1984). Revision of the self-monitoring scale. *Journal of Personality and Social Psychology, 46*, 1349-1364.

Levine, D. (1985). *The flight from ambiguity*. Chicago: University of Chicago Press.

LeVine, R. A., & Campbell, D. T. (1972). *Ethnocentrism: Theories of conflict, ethnic attitudes, and group behavior*. New York: John Wiley.

Loveday, L. (1982). Communicative interference. *International Review of Applied Linguistics in Language Teaching, 20*, 1-16.

Lukens, J. (1978). Ethnocentric speech. *Ethnic Groups, 2*, 35-53.

Lynberg, M. (1989). *The path with heart*. New York: Fawcett.

McArthur, L. (1982). Judging a book by its cover. In A. Hastorf & A. Isen (Eds.), *Cognitive social psychology*. New York: Elsevier-North Nolland.

McConahay, J. B. (1986). Modern racism, ambivalence, and the modern racism scale. In J. Dovidio & S. Gaertner (Eds.), *Prejudice, discrimination, and racism*. New York: Academic Press.

McFall, R. (1982). A review and reformulation of the concept of social skills. *Behavioral Assessment, 4*, 1-33.

McGinn, N., Harburg, E., & Ginsburg, G. (1973). Responses to interpersonal conflict by middle class males in Guadalajara and Michigan. In F. Jandt (Ed.), *Conflict resolution through communication*. New York: Harper & Row.

McKirnan, D., & Hamayan, E. (1984). Speech norms and perceptions of ethnolinguistic group differences. *European Journal of Social Psychology, 14*, 151-168.

McLeod, J., & Chaffee, S. (1973). Interpersonal approach to communication research. *American Behavioral Scientist, 16*, 469-499.

McPherson, K. (1983). Opinion-related information seeking. *Personality and Social Psychology Bulletin, 9*, 116-124.

Messick, D., & Mackie, D. (1989). Intergroup relations. *Annual Review of Psychology, 40*, 45-81.

Miller, G., & Steinberg, M. (1975). *Between people*. Chicago: Science Research Associates.

Miller, G., & Sunnafrank, M. (1982). All is for one but one is not for all. In F. Dance (Ed.), *Human communication theory*. New York: Harper & Row.

Miller, J. (1984). Culture and the development of everyday social explanations. *Journal of Personality and Social Psychology, 46*, 961-978.

Nakane, C. (1970). *Japanese society*. Berkeley: University of California Press.

Neuberg, S. (1989). The goal of forming accurate impressions during initial interactions. *Journal of Personality and Social Psychology, 56*, 374-386.

Noller, P. (1980). Misunderstandings in marital communication. *Journal of Personality and Social Psychology, 39*, 1135-1148.

Nozick, R. (1989). *The examined life*. New York: Simon and Schuster.

Ogden, C., & Richards, I. (1923). *The meaning of meaning*. New York: Harcourt, Brace.

Olsen, M. (1978). *The process of social organization* (2nd ed.). New York: Holt, Rinehart, & Winston.

Optow, S. (1990). Moral exclusion and injustice: An introduction. *Journal of Social Issues, 46* (1), 1-20.

Park, R. E. (1950). Our racial frontier in the Pacific. In R. Park (Ed.), *Race and culture*. New York: Free Press.

Peck, M. S. (1987). *The different drum: Community making and peace*. New York: Simon & Schuster.

Pettigrew, T. F. (1958). The measurement and correlates of category width as a cognitive variable. *Journal of Personality, 26*, 532-544.

Pettigrew, T. F. (1978). Three issues in ethnicity. In Y. Yinger & S. Cutler (Eds.), *Major social issues*. New York: Free Press.

Pettigrew, T. F. (1979). The ultimate attribution error. *Personality and Social Psychology Bulletin, 5*, 461-476.

Pettigrew, T. F. (1982). Cognitive styles and social behavior. In L. Wheeler (Ed.), *Review of personality and social psychology* (Vol. 3). Beverly Hills, CA: Sage.

Powers, W., & Lowrey, D. (1984). Basic communication fidelity. In R. Bostrom (Ed.), *Competence in communication*. Beverly Hills, CA: Sage.

Prather, H. (1986). *Notes on how to live in the world and still be happy*. Garden City, NY: Doubleday.

Pyszczynski, T., & Greenberg, J. (1981). Role of disconfirmed expectancies in the instigation of attributional processing. *Journal of Personality and Social Psychology, 40*, 31-38.

Roach, C., & Wyatt, N. (1988). *Successful listening*. New York: Harper & Row.

Rodriguez, R. (1982). *Hunger of memory*. New York: Bantam.

Rokeach, M. (1951). A method for studying individual differences in "narrow-mindedness." *Journal of Personality, 20*, 219-233.

Rogers, C. (1980). *A way of being*. Boston: Houghton Mifflin.

Rogers, E., & Kincaid, D. L. (1981). *Communication networks*. New York: Free Press.

Roosens, E. (1989). *Creating ethnicity*. Newbury Park, CA: Sage.

Rose, T. (1981). Cognitive and dyadic processes in intergroup contact. In D. Hamilton (Ed.), *Cognitive processes in stereotyping and intergroup behavior*. Hillsdale, NJ: Lawrence Erlbaum.

Rosenthal, P. (1984). *Words and values*. Cambridge, UK: Cambridge University Press.

Ross, L. (1977). The intuitive psychologist and his shortcomings. *Advances in Experimental and Social Psychology, 10*, 174-220.

Ruben, B. (1976). Assessing communication competency for intercultural adaptation. *Group and Organizational Studies, 1*, 334-354.

Ruben, B., & Kealey, D. (1979). Behavioral assessment of communication competency and the prediction of cross-cultural adaptation. *International Journal of Intercultural Relations, 3*, 15-48.

Rubin, T. I. (1990). *Anti-Semitism: A disease of the mind*. New York: Continuum.

Saleh, S., & Gufwoli, P. (1982). The transfer of management techniques and practices: The Kenya case. In R. Rath et al. (Eds.), *Diversity and unity in cross-cultural psychology*. Lisse, The Netherlands: Swets & Zeitlinger.

Satir, V. (1967). *Cojoint family therapy* (rev. ed.). Palo Alto, CA: Science & Behavior Books.

Schwartz, J. (1980). The negotiation for meaning. In D. Larsen-Freeman (Ed.), *Discourse analysis in second language research*. Rowley, MA: Newbury House.

Schwartz, S. (1990). Individualism-collectivism: Critique and proposed refinements. *Journal of Cross-Cultural Psychology, 21*, 139-157.

Scotton, C. (1980). Explaining linguistic choices as identity negotiations. In H. Giles, P. Robinson, & P. Smith (Eds.), *Language: Social psychological perspectives*. Oxford, UK: Pergamon.

Slobin, L., Collins, M., Crayton, J., Feldman, J., Jaccard, J., Rissman, K., & Weldon, D. (1972). *Culture assimilator: For interaction with the economically disadvantaged* (Vol. 1). Department of Psychology, University of Illinois (available from National Technical Information Service, Springfield, VA).

Skevington, S. (1989). A place for emotion in social identity theory. In S. Skevington & D. Baker (Eds.), *The social identity of women*. London: Sage.

Skevington, S., & Baker, D. (Eds.). (1989). *The social identity of women*. London: Sage.

Smith, S., & Whitehead, G. (1984). Attributions for promotions and demotions in the United States and India. *The Journal of Social Psychology, 124*, 27-34.

Snyder, M. (1974). Self-monitoring of expressive behavior. *Journal of Personality and Social Psychology, 30*, 526-537.

Sorrentino, R. M., & Short, J. A. (1986). Uncertainty orientation, motivation, and cognition. In R. M. Sorrentino & E. T. Higgins (Eds.), *Handbook of motivation and cognition*. New York: Guilford.

Spitzberg, B., & Cupach, W. (1984). *Interpersonal communication competence*. Beverly Hills, CA: Sage.

Stephan, W. G. (1985). Intergroup relations. In G. Lindzey & E. Aronson (Eds.), *Handbook of social psychology* (3rd ed., Vol. 2). New York: Random House.

Stephan, W. G., & Rosenfield, D. (1982). Racial and ethnic stereotyping. In A. Millar (Ed.), *In the eye of the beholder*. New York: Praeger.

Stephan, W. G., & Stephan, C. W. (1985). Intergroup anxiety. *Journal of Social Issues, 41*, 157-166.

Stephan, W. G., & Stephan, C. W. (1989). Antecedents of intergroup anxiety in Asian-Americans and Hispanic-Americans. *International Journal of Intercultural Relations, 13*, 203-219.

Stewart, J. (1990). Interpersonal communication. In J. Stewart (Ed.), *Bridges not walls* (5th ed.). New York: McGraw-Hill.

Stewart, J., & Thomas, M. (1990). Dialogic listening. In J. Stewart (Ed.), *Bridges not walls* (5th ed.). New York: McGraw-Hill.

Strobe, W., Kruglanski, A., Bar-Tal, D., & Hewstone, M. (Eds.). 1988). *The social psychology of intergroup conflict.* New York: Springer-Verlag.

Sudweeks, S., Gudykunst, W. B., Nishida, T., & Ting-Toomey, S. (1990). Relational themes in Japanese-North American relationships. *International Journal of Intercultural Relations, 14,* 207-233.

Sumner, W. G. (1940). *Folkways.* Boston: Ginn Press.

Tajfel, H. (1978). Social categorization, social identity, and social comparisons. In H. Tajfel (Ed.), *Differentiation between social groups.* London: Academic Press.

Tajfel, H. (1981). Social stereotypes and social groups. In J. Turner & H. Giles (Eds.), *Intergroup behavior.* Chicago: University of Chicago Press.

Tajfel, H., & Turner, J. (1979). An integrative theory of intergroup conflict. In W. Austin & S. Worchel (Eds.), *The social psychology of intergroup relations.* Monterey, CA: Brooks/Cole.

Tannen, D. (1979). Ethnicity as conversational style. In *Working papers in sociolinguistics* (Number 55). Austin, TX: Southwest Educational Development Laboratory.

Tannen, D. (1990). *You just don't understand: Women and men in conversation.* New York: William Morrow.

Tempest, R. (1990, June 12). Hate survives a holocaust: Anti-Semitism resurfaces. *Los Angeles Times,* pp. H1, H7.

Thomas, K. (1983). Conflict and its management. In M. Dunnette (Ed.), *Handbook of industrial and organizational psychology.* New York: John Wiley.

Tinder, G. (1980). *Community: Reflections on a tragic ideal.* Baton Rouge: Louisiana State University Press.

Ting-Toomey, S. (1985). Toward a theory of conflict and culture. In W. Gudykunst, L. Stewart, & S. Ting-Toomey (Eds.), *Communication, culture, and organizational processes.* Beverly Hills, CA: Sage.

Ting-Toomey, S. (1986). Conflict styles in black and white subjective cultures. In Y. Kim (Ed.), *Current research in interethnic communication.* Beverly Hills, CA: Sage.

Ting-Toomey, S. (1988). A face negotiation theory. In Y. Kim & W. Gudykunst (Ed.), *Theories in intercultural communication.* Newbury Park, CA: Sage.

Ting-Toomey, S. (1989). Identity and interpersonal bonding. In M. Asante & W. Gudykunst (Eds.), *Handbook of international and intercultural communication.* Newbury Park, CA: Sage.

Triandis, H. C. (1975). Culture training, cognitive complexity, and interpersonal attitudes. In R. Brislin, S. Bochner, & W. Lonner (Eds.), *Cross-cultural perspectives on learning.* Beverly Hills, CA: Sage.

Triandis, H. C. (1977). *Interpersonal behavior.* Monterey, CA: Brooks/Cole.

Triandis, H. C. (1980). Values, attitudes, and interpersonal behavior. In M. Page (Ed.), *Nebraska symposium on motivation* (Vol. 27). Lincoln: University of Nebraska Press.

Triandis, H. C. (1983). Essentials of studying culture. In D. Landis & R. Brislin (Eds.), *Handbook of intercultural training* (Vol. 1). Elmsford, NY: Pergamon.

Triandis, H. C. (1988). Collectivism vs. individualism. In G. Verma & C. Bagley (Eds.), *Cross-cultural studies of personality, attitudes, and cognition*. London: Macmillan.

Triandis, H. C., Brislin, R., & Hui, C. H. (1988). Cross-cultural training across the individualism-collectivism divide. *International Journal of Intercultural Relations, 12,* 269-289.

Triandis, H. C., Leung, K., Villareal, M., & Clack, F. (1985). Allocentric vs. idiocentric tendencies. *Journal of Research in Personality, 19,* 395-415.

Trilling, L. (1968). *Beyond culture*. New York: Viking Press.

Trungpa, C. (1973). *Cutting through spiritual materialism*. Boulder, CO: Shambhala.

Turner, J. C. (1982). Towards a cognitive redefinition of the social group. In H. Tajfel (Ed.), *Social identity and intergroup relations*. Cambridge, UK: Cambridge University Press.

Turner, J. C. (1987). *Rediscovering the social group*. Oxford, UK: Basil Blackwell.

Turner, J. H. (1987). Toward a sociological theory of motivation. *American Sociological Review, 52,* 15-27.

van Dijk, T. (1984). *Prejudice in discourse*. Amsterdam: Benjamins.

Varonis, E., & Gass, S. (1985). Nonnative/native conversations: A model for negotiation of meaning. *Applied Linguistics, 6,* 71-90.

Vassiliou, V., Triandis, H. C., Vassiliou, G., & McGuire, H. (1972). Interpersonal contact and stereotyping. In H. Triandis (Ed.), *Analysis of subjective culture*. New York: John Wiley.

Vlastos, G. (in press). *Socrates, ironist and moral philosopher*. Ithaca, NY: Cornell University Press.

Waterman, A. (1984). *The psychology of individualism*. New York: Praeger.

Watzlawick, P., Beavin, J., & Jackson, D. (1967). *The pragmatics of human communication*. New York: Norton.

Wiemann, J. M., & Backlund, P. (1980). Current theory and research in communication competence. *Review of Educational Research, 50,* 185-199.

Wiemann, J. M., & Bradac, J. (1989). Metatheoretical issues in the study of communicative competence. In B. Dervin (Ed.), *Progress in communication sciences* (Vol. 9). Norwood, NJ: Ablex.

Wiemann, J. M., & Kelly, C. (1981). Pragmatics of interpersonal competence. In C. Wilder-Mott & J. Weaklund (Eds.), *Rigor and imagination*. New York: Praeger.

Williams, J. (1984). Gender and intergroup behavior. *British Journal of Social Psychology, 23,* 311-316.

Worchel, S., & Norwell, N. (1980). Effect of perceived environmental conditions during co-operation on intergroup attraction. *Journal of Personality and Social Psychology, 38,* 764-772.

Yankelovich, D. (1981). *New rules: Searching for self-fulfillment in a world turned upside down*. New York: Random House.

Zajonc, R. (1980). Feeling and thinking. *American Psychologist, 35,* 151-175.

Name Index

Subject Index

About the Author

William B. Gudykunst is Professor of Speech Communication at California State University, Fullerton. Over the past 10 years he has been working to generate a theory of interpersonal and intergroup communication that generalizes across cultures. He applies the most recent version of the theory to improving effectiveness in communicating with strangers in this volume. His other books include *Culture and Interpersonal Communication* (with Stella Ting-Toomey) and *Communicating with Strangers* (with Young Yun Kim). In addition, he has edited or co-edited numerous books, including *Intercultural Communication Theory, Intergroup Communication, Theories of Intercultural Communication* (with Young Yun Kim), and *Handbook of International and Intercultural Communication* (with Molefi Asante), among others. Currently he is working on a second edition of *Communicating with Strangers* (with Young Yun Kim) and a reader to accompany the text *Readings on Communicating with Strangers* (with Young Yun Kim), as well as a theoretical monograph summarizing the theory he has been developing.

NOTES